PARALLAX

STEVEN HOLL

PARALLAX

DESIGNED BY 2x4, NEW YORK

PRINCETON ARCHITECTURAL PRESS, NEW YORK

Published by
Princeton Architectural Press
37 East 7th Street
New York, New York 10003

For a free catalog of books, call 1.800.722.6657.
Visit our web site at www.papress.com.

Editing: Clare Jacobson

Special thanks to: Ann Alter, Amanda Atkins, Nicola Bednarek, Eugenia Bell, Jan Cigliano,
Jane Garvie, Caroline Green, Beth Harrison, Mia Ihara, Leslie Ann Kent, Mark Lamster,
Anne Nitschke, Lottchen Shivers, Jennifer Thompson, and Deb Wood of Princeton
Architectural Press—Kevin C. Lippert, publisher

Holl, Steven.
     Parallax / Steven Holl.
          p. cm.
     ISBN 1-56898-261-5 (alk. paper)
          1. Holl, Steven—Themes, motives. 2. Architecture, Modern—20th century—United
     States—Themes, motives. I. Title.

NA737.H56 A4 2000
720'.92—dc21

00-037325

ACKNOWLEDGMENTS

This book affirms a spirit in architecture and discoveries in science and perception, and tries to explore the relation of one to the other. Illustrated with recent architectural projects (a practicing architect's revelation!), it is a book of questions without overt concern for academic discourse. Sentences in the text are almost always short. Schisms are intentionally left as break-out points for the reader.

Thanks to the invitation of Bruce Mau and the Powerplant in Toronto this text began as a lecture given on May 11, 1999. Critical help from Michael Bell as well as remarks from Alberto Perez Gomez, Kenneth Frampton, Lebbeus Woods, Guy Nordenson, Madeline Gins, Sandro Marpiellero, Paola Iaccuci, Janet Cross, Yehuda Safran, and Andrew MacNair have been instrumental. Michael Rock and 2x4 have contributed more than graphic design. I would also like to thank Chris McVoy, Aislinn Weidele, and the artist Solange Fabião, whose brilliant eye is evident in several of the photographs.

Steven Holl
5/8/00 New York City

ELASTIC HORIZONS

For over thirty years, emerging discoveries in science have stretched earth-bound horizons. Since Neil Armstrong's 1969 walk on the moon, we have viewed the Earth from a curved, dusty horizon. A more expansive knowledge of horizons beyond the Earth should not lead to a more diminished expectation for the Earth's tangible experiences. The inexpressible harmony of this world comes with a new organic understanding of dynamic systems. Microbiological discoveries and methods correlate with the cosmological. Evolution brings fractal, contingent, interactive, and combinative forms and methods. As a new template to understand space, our recharged perception offers new ideas to the spatial imagination.

Elasticity can be defined as a new malleable inner horizon in fragmented boundaries of tension, condensation, and expansion that challenge thought. In the twenty-first century, the horizons of our fundamental experiences have expanded and continue to expand. We experience and think differently, therefore we feel differently. How elastic are our minds? How far can we stretch them?

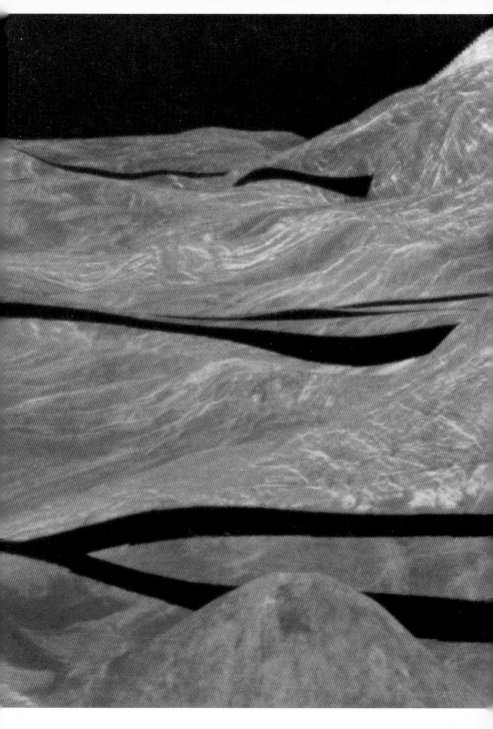

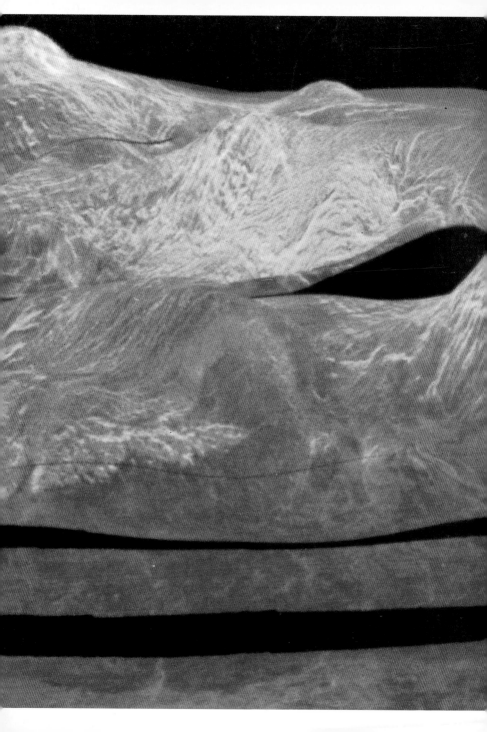

Perception is altered by science's spatial discoveries. New views of
intergalactic space stretch psychological space. Experience is understood
not only via objects or things, yet space is only perceived when a subject
describes it. As that subject occupies a particular time, space is thus
linked to a perceived duration. The virtual body, as a system of nerves and
senses, is "oriented" in space. It is either upside down or right side up.
The body is at the very essence of our being and our spatial perception.
As we move through spaces, the body moves in a constant state of
essential incompletion. A determinate point of view necessarily gives way
to an indeterminate flow of perspectives. The spectacle of spatial flow
is continuously alive in the metropolis, as well as throughout the world.
It creates an exhilaration, which nourishes the emergence of tentative
meanings from the inside. Perception and cognition balance the volumetrics
of architectural spaces with the understanding of time itself. An ecstatic
architecture of the immeasurable emerges. It is precisely at the level of
spatial perception that the most powerful architectural meanings come
to the fore.

Surface of Venus seen from the cloud-piercing radar of *Magellan*

Light has a new prolific dimension today as a means of measurement and communication. Compared to the speed of light, all the tangible motions involved in our day-to-day experiences on Earth are tremendously slow. Sound travels at a relatively slow speed of 700 miles per hour compared to light, which travels 186,000 miles per second—the difference is so great that it is almost incomparable. The two fundamental theories of modern physics, general relativity (for the large scale) and quantum mechanics (for the smallest scales), are not yet reconcilable. Science remains essentially mysterious, yet our daily scientific and phenomenal experiences shape our lives; experience sets a new frame from which we interpret what we perceive.

Curtains of light: electrons from the solar wind rain down along the Earth's magnetic field lines. Color depends on the type of atom or molecule struck by the charged particles. The northern lights or aurora borealis are historically poetic and mythical—today full of new feelings.

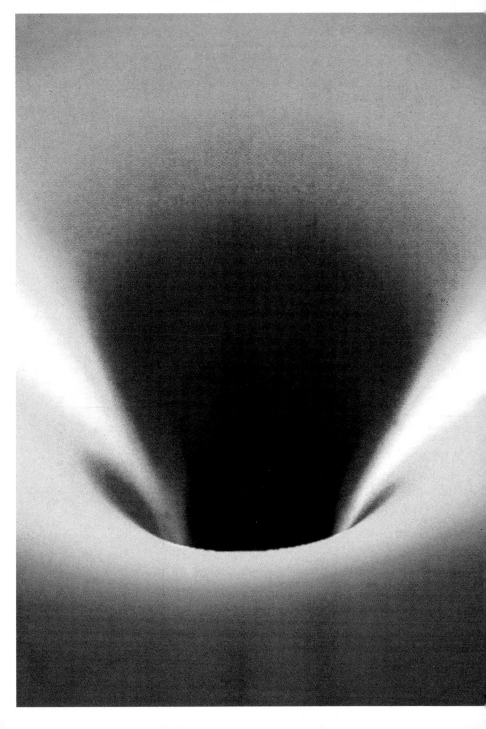

In the mist of the metropolis at night, space dissolves before our eyes, only to take shape again within seconds. The spatial depth of the urban field cannot be objectified precisely. In its pulse the polarized position of our body and its perceptions are upset. If we explore spatial depth, then we can consider how objects appear correct or inverted. During our thought-experiments regarding space—especially space beyond the earthbound—we accept new spatial levels and, by the force of our imaginations, alter the known spatial levels of previous human existence.

Consider recent discussions of the behavior of a black hole in a galaxy 100 million light years away. Scientists estimate the capability of a black hole to pull matter in at a speed of six million miles per hour. The outer limit of a black hole, the realm of no escape for matter and light, is called the "event horizon." For example, the event horizon of a black hole 800 times the mass of the sun is roughly 3000 miles in diameter (the distance from New York to Los Angeles). The term "horizon" is open to new limits and new meanings with unforeseen discoveries.

Event horizon, black hole

A horizon is not only an optical condition but also a spinning moment in space-time. In this sense, the earth is not the ground. As things continue to float, they spin and accelerate. Centrifugal forces—like electronic loops with steel sword blades—propel centripetal grounds. The mechanical gives way to diverse, digitally dynamic systems. Still, we are organic beings. All of our objective relations begin from the inside out. We must form an extended comprehension of space and time at the scale of astronomical events while not losing the perspective of the microscopic.

Horizon with aurora borealis

Horizons of thought—ever larger, more expanded, incorporating rotations and energies—seek to reconcile the microscopic and the ecological dimensions contracting an earth-bound crisis. As the horizon of our globe contracts, the horizon of our thought expands. In the face of immeasurable transformations in thought, our values at every scale stand to be redefined.

A radarsat satellite allows us to see the Earth in a new way. A view of Antarctica's Lake Vostok; 140 miles by 30 miles wide with liquid sealed from view for over a million years.

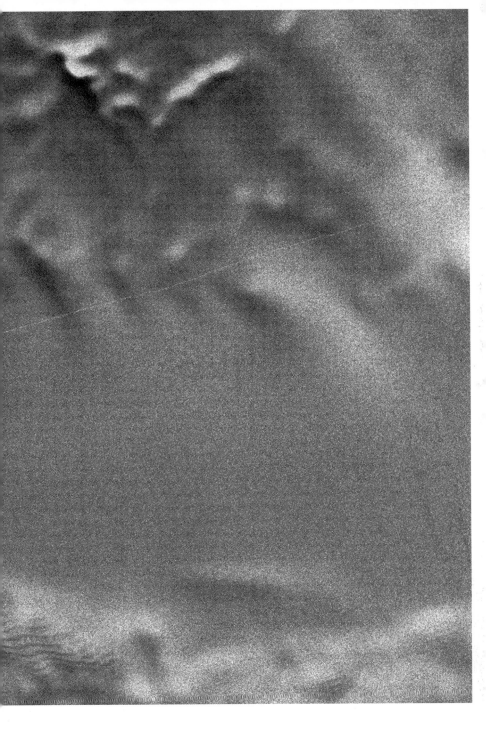

CRISS-CROSSING

"For a building to be motionless is the exception: our pleasure comes from moving about so as to make the building move in turn, while we enjoy all these combinations of its parts. As they vary, the column turns, depths recede, galleries glide: a thousand visions escape."

—Paul Valéry, *The Method of Leonardo*

Space is the essential medium of architecture. Space is simultaneously many things—the voids in architecture, the space around architecture, the vast space of landscape and city space, intergalactic spaces of the universe. Space is something both intrinsic and relational.

Stretto House, Dallas, Texas, 1991

Kiasma Museum of Contemporary Art, Helsinki, Finland, 1998
Space curves turning the vanishing point

Parallax—the change in the arrangement of surfaces that define space as a result of the change in the position of a viewer—is transformed when movement axes leave the horizontal dimension. Vertical or oblique movements through urban space multiply our experiences. Spatial definition is ordered by angles of perception. The historical idea of perspective as enclosed volumetrics based on horizontal space gives way today to the vertical dimension. Architectural experience has been taken out of its historical closure. Vertical and oblique slippages are key to new spatial perceptions.

The movement of the body as it crosses through overlapping perspectives formed within spaces is the elemental connection between ourselves and architecture. The "apparent horizon" is a determining factor in the moving body's interpretation of space; yet the modern metropolis often lacks this horizon. Sequential experiences of space in parallax, with its luminous flux, can only be played out in personal perception. There is no more important measure of the force and potential of architecture. If we allow magazine photos or screen images to replace experience, our ability to perceive architecture will diminish so greatly that it will become impossible to comprehend it. Our faculty of judgment is incomplete without this experience of crossing through spaces. The turn and twist of the body engaging a long and then a short perspective, an up-and-down movement, an open-and-closed or dark-and-light rhythm of geometries—these are the core of the spatial score of architecture.

Parallax has taken astronomy out of the solar system.

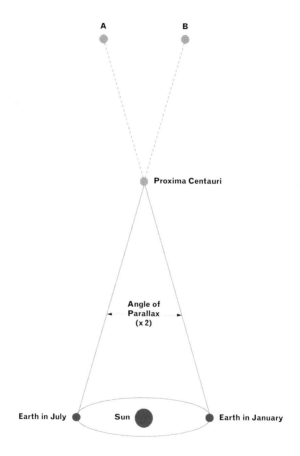

A   B

Proxima Centauri

Angle of
Parallax
(x 2)

Earth in July   Sun   Earth in January

1992 watercolor from the Kiasma competition

From the series "Unique in Architectural Time," Kiasma 1997

The edges, contours, and surfaces of the structures that define urban spaces (redefined in parallax) are revealed in dynamic perception and in light. Mere geometry or the idea of "facade" is too limiting. The experience of urban space generated by the slight rotation of individual planar walls is inseparable from the parabola of sunlight grazing its boundaries. The movement of sunlight exerts relational forces on spatial definition, engaging the body of a stationary building. The silver light of the sun, the tree-cast shadow, and the glossy surface of concrete walls interact in a shadow play with the body's movement through them.

City spaces at night embrace us with ellipses of projected light, glowing glass facades, and transformations induced by mists and rain. A dense complex of blocks, cut by a canyon street by day, is redefined by night as a shimmering prism of lights in a chiaroscuro of projected shadows. There are astonishing effects of fog vapors at night when clouds of white light surround the tops of lighted towers, or golden gauzelike ribbons radiate into the night sky. The spatial definitions of the city interlock in a web of movement, parallax, and light.

We play in unqualified delight with our eyes open, our legs moving, our arms and torso engaged. The phenomenon of ineffable space refers to the maximum intensity and the quality of execution and proportion—an experience becomes radiant. Dimensions alone do not create this space; rather the space is a quality bound up in perception.

Kiasma with the Parliament Building. Urban experience is a series of partial views. Every angle slices a different geometry.

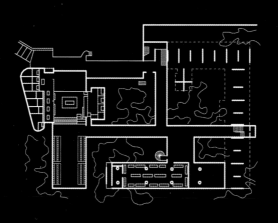

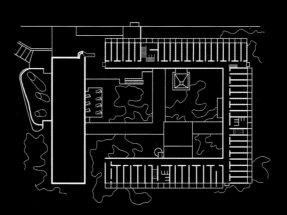

Le Corbusier's La Tourette at Eveux-sur-l'Arbresle best exemplifies his concept of "ineffable space." This intense little city was designed in 1953 and inaugurated on October 19, 1960. On my first visit to La Tourette in April 1976, I stayed three days in one of the cells, making drawings and measurements. Revisiting on August 29, 1999, I discovered new qualities of this intense work, qualities I had not noticed twenty-three years before. The three sides of the square plan are bound to the church on the fourth by a cruciform cloister. The whole complex begins with the upper horizon of the top floor and, except for the church, is suspended without "sitting" on the earth. The courtyard, with a pyramid oratory instead of a fountain, is the only apparent center of gravity for the complex. The church, a pure, blank, oblong rectangle, has choir stalls built parallel to the main long axis that passes through the high altar. A second, more mysterious, central crossing connects below the altar from the sacristy into the crypt. Here, passing nearly blind in the darkness of the tunnel, is the main criss-crossing in the complex—not the assumed one in the central cloister. Le Corbusier gives this obscure crossing the most pronounced geometry in the complex. It begins in the seven trapezoidal light cannons over the sacristy, and, after the disorienting tunnel passage, ends in the three luminous oval light cannons over the stepped ramp floor of the crypt. Here is liquid space with an undulating inclined wall. As a metaphorical journey towards a personal revelation, it shows the dimension of an inner discovery in its unexpectedness. While the architecture appears from the exterior as convent-square, it yields an interior of astonishing curvilinear experiences.

Left: Plans of level 2 and level 5, La Tourette, l'Arbresle, 1960

atrium and moving up and down along the Xenakis-drawn music of the shadow-strewn ramps—become part of the dimension that teases, jokes, and excites. The stair tower diagonally opposite the bell tower juts up in a tiny, narrow space with a dynamic, square-spiraling window that looks onto the grassy landscape of the walled garden roof. One hangs behind the locked door like the bell in the tower across the complex. La Tourette now functions as the Thomas Moore Center to promote research of the problems of human existence, but this architectural vessel, with all its secret dimensions and inspiring force, is open to teach eternal lessons.

Liquid space, La Tourette, sketch, 1999

Arriving at the top gallery after a sequence of 25 galleries, all with a different natural light

In *The Intertwining, The Chiasma*, Merleau-Ponty writes, "Through this criss-crossing within it of the touching and the tangible, its own movements incorporate themselves into the universe they interrogate." The body incorporates and describes the world. Motility and the body-subject are the instruments for measuring architectural space. Mundane phenomenological studies are as ineffectual as an overdose of wide-angle, distorted color photography. Only the criss-crossing of the body through space—like connecting electric currents—joins space, body, eye, and mind.

The Helsinki Museum of Contemporary Art, "Kiasma," argues for the body to be the real measure of overlapping space. The criss-crossing of the building concept and an intertwining of the landscape, light, and the city mark many routes through the museum that involve turns of the body and the parallax of unfolding spaces. The body becomes a living spatial measure in moving through the outstretched, overlapping perspectives. The encompassing space forms an escape from the dualities of body/thing and man/nature in a doubling back and crossing over. The geometry folds into itself in order to transcend the body/person or space/object relation.

The facade expresses shear; its two sides are shifted—left side out, right side in—to begin the chiasmatic intertwining of the spaces beyond. Thus, the spatial criss-crossing joins with a criss-crossing of the seer and the seen, the tangible and the visible.

Initial watercolor concept sketch made in Helsinki, October 10, 1992

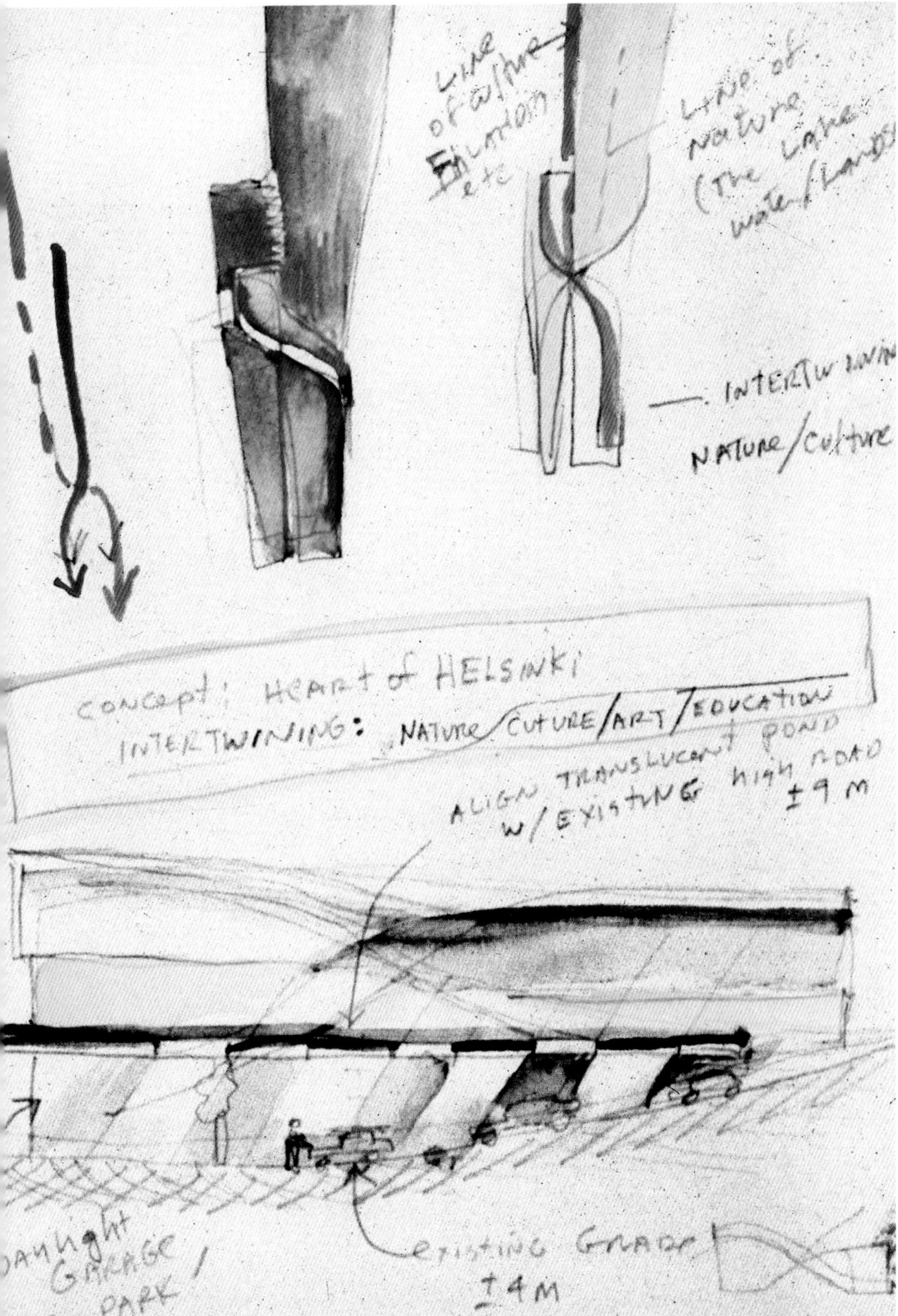

Line of culture Education etc

Line of nature (The Lake water flants

—— INTERTWINING
NATURE/CULTURE

CONCEPT: HEART of HELSINKI

INTERTWINING: NATURE/CULTURE/ART/EDUCATION

ALIGN TRANSLUCENT POND
w/ EXISTING HIGH ROAD ±9 M

DAYLIGHT GARAGE / PARK!

EXISTING GRADE ±4 M

The facade expresses shear, left side out, right side in.

Computer sketch that provoked the idea of going from mass directly to detail, with no
intermediate scale, 1992

Kiasma curved space study, 1992

11
30
93

At the building's entrance, space curves, vanishing points disappear. Here the human figure can be seen in at least three levels due to the upper ramps—the space comes alive with the body-subject. This vast spatial curve is activated from several points of view and several "horizons."

Left: Sketch of the upper ramp added after the competition

Below: Change of parallactic angle with altitude

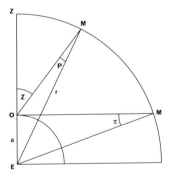

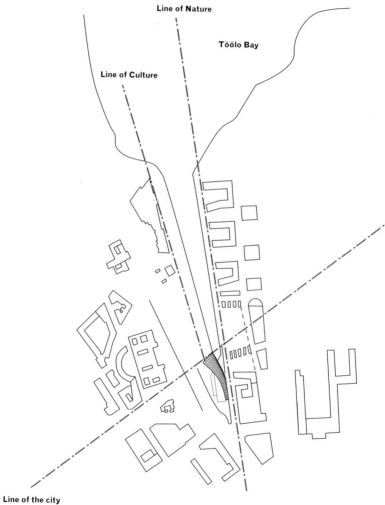

Line of Nature

Töölo Bay

Line of Culture

Line of the city

Upper ramp, Kiasma: the body in space at three levels in motion

At the chiasmatic crossing where the two main building forms fold into a cross passage, the vertical intersection is defined by **DNA**-like, vertical ribbons of concrete stairs warping into connections of all the levels. The visitor's choice of multiple circuits through the galleries emphasizes this crossing.

In the galleries, orthogonal, neutral walls are slightly warped by the overall building geometry that pulls the viewer through space. The entire sequence of twenty-five galleries—all with some degree of natural light—ends like a musical sequence in a grand, upper-level gallery that seems to billow out, light blowing from the western "wall of ice." **K**iasma is a space for contemporary art, necessarily a dynamic unfolding phenomena.

Left: **DNA**-like stair connecting all levels at chiasmatic crossing

Below: **U**tilizing the unique properties of natural light in a 60° north latitude, the primary curvature of the building forms a reversal of the sun path.

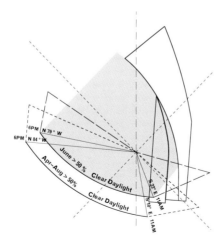

Light blowing the space from the "wall of ice"

ENMESHED EXPERIENCE

The experience of architecture transcends that of the cinema. It has all-encompassing qualities. From the optic-haptic realm of material and detail to the connections of space developed in the light of foreground, middle ground, and distant view, architecture is manifest in perception. Enmeshed experience, or the merging of object and field, is an elemental force of architecture.

Beyond the physicality of architectural objects and the necessities of programmatic content, enmeshed experience is not merely a place of events, things, and activities, but a more intangible condition that emerges from the continuous unfolding of overlapping spaces, materials, and detail. This "in-between reality" is analogous to the moment in which individual elements begin to lose their clarity, the moment in which an object merges with its field.

From filmmaker Andrei Tarkovsky's "sculpting in time"

From touching the smallest detail to sensing the movement of a body and its acceleration in space—all of these sensations criss-cross in the chemistry of things, spontaneously developing in a play of natural light toward the distant horizon. A phenomenological enmeshing of object-side and subject-side, which is most readily achieved in architecture, points beyond itself.

"Our fields merge, overlap and are doubly articulated. The senses are fields."

—Maurice Merleau-Ponty

"Y" House, Schohari County, New York, 1999, nothing in the distance. In his 1952 "Lecture on Nothing," John Cage wrote, "Something and nothing are not opposed to each other but need each other to keep going on."

As a detail of a lamp merges with a steel handrail, which in turn merges with the horizontal sunlight of a large space, individual elements blur and the overall enmeshed experience approaches the strange and transcendent.

The architectural synthesis of foreground, middle ground, and distant view, together with all the subjective qualities of material and light, form the basis of complete perception. The expression of the originating idea is a fusion of the subjective and objective. The conceptual logic that drives a design is linked to its ultimate perception.

Detail at "Y" House. Steel channel's intentional gap against distant horizon.

When we sit in a room at a desk by a window, the distant view, the light from the window, the floor material, the wood of the desk, and the eraser in our hand begin to merge perceptually. The overlap of foreground, middle ground, and distant view is a critical issue in the creation of architectural space. We must consider space, light, color, geometry, detail, and material as an experimental continuum. Though we can disassemble these elements and study them individually during the design process, they merge in the final condition, and ultimately we cannot readily break perception into a simple collection of geometries, activities, and sensations.

The sky is broken, the clouds fold, inner space rises to the distant horizon

A complex interlocking of time, light, material, and detail creates the cinematic whole wherein we can no longer distinguish individual elements. Filmmaker Andrey Tarkovsky speaks of cinematic enmeshing in his description of a scene from Akira Kurosawa's *The Seven Samurai*, "A medieval Japanese village. A fight is going on between some horsemen and the samurai who are on foot. It is pouring rain; there is mud everywhere. The samurai wears an ancient Japanese garment, which leaves more of the leg bare, and their arms are plastered in mud. And, when one samurai falls down dead, we see the rain washing away the mud and his leg becoming white, as white as marble."

Section splits to advance toward two views of the horizon. Functions are day over night on left, and night over day on right.

CHEMISTRY OF MATTER
(FROM IMAGE TO THE HAPTIC REALM)

"The surface of bread is marvelous, first of all, because of the almost
panoramic impression it gives: as though you held the Alps...the Andes
in your hand."

—Francis Ponge

The smell of rain-wet dirt, the texture merged with the color and the
fragrance of orange rinds, and the steel-iced fusion of cold and hard:
these shape the haptic realm. The essences of material, smell, texture,
temperature, and touch vitalize everyday existence.

Phenomenology is a discipline that puts essences into experience. The
complete perception of architecture depends on the material and detail
of the haptic realm, as the taste of a meal depends on the flavors of its
ingredients. As one can imagine being condemned to eating only artificially
flavored foods, so one can imagine the specter of artificially constituted
surroundings imposing themselves in architecture today.

800-year-old stave church in Norway, coated with tar from peat bogs

My recent stay at a Ramada Inn in the Midwest began in a lobby with no natural light (blank walls to a parking lot), which led to a confusing series of Sheetrock-lined, carpeted, double-loaded corridors that smelled of perfumed cleaning fluid. Finally, the wood-grained Formica door opened to a polyester-carpeted "large" room with vinyl wallpaper and an acoustic-panel ceiling. Though the smell was stifling, the anodized aluminum window was not operable. Synthetic (and sometimes toxic) interiors of typical lodgings scattered in polluted landscapes characterize today's throw-away environment.

As a catalyst for change, architecture's ability to shape our daily experiences in material and detail is subtle yet powerful. When sensory experience is intensified, psychological dimensions are engaged.

Beeswax-covered Chapel of the Blessed Sacrament, Chapel of St. Ignatius, Seattle, Washington, 1997; olfactory space.

Electron microscope view of dust mites grazing

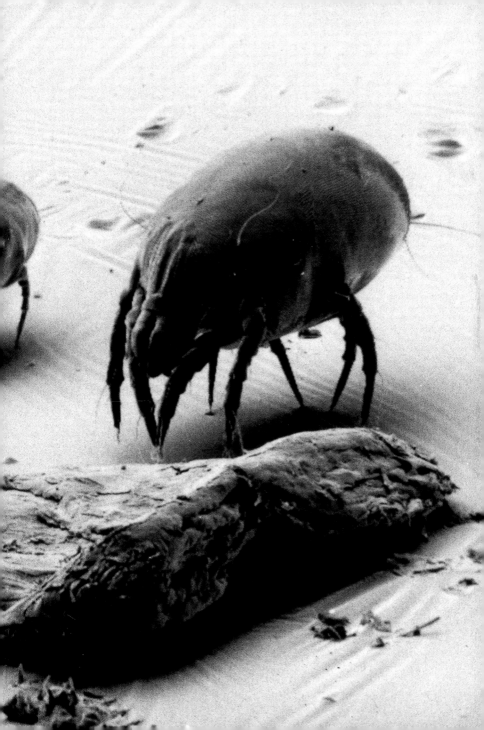

Materials may be altered through a variety of new means, which may even enhance their natural properties. For example, new developments in translucent insulation have given a new life to structural glass plank systems developed over forty years ago. The translucent insulation in white glass planks that constitute the west wall of the Helsinki Museum of Contemporary Art allows for new hybrid techniques.

Glass becomes radiant in transformed states, while its functional role shifts. Bending glass induces dazzling variations to a simple plane with the curvature of reflected light. Cast glass with its mysterious opacity traps light in its mass and projects a diffused glow. Sandblasted glass likewise has a luminescence, which changes subtly depending on the glass type, thickness, and blasting method. The silicone bead blasting or acid etching of glass traps light and creates an obscure glow. The chrome, glass, and glossy granite used in so many modern lobbies mirror a brash light and an intimidating mood, while cloudy sandblasted glass and honed materials establish a material depth, a pensive mood.

Metals can also be significantly transformed by sandblasting, bending, and oxidizing to create rich surface textures and colors. A variety of metals such as copper, nickel, and zinc can be electronically atomized and sprayed in a layer over the surface of a different material, thus opening up possibilities for the strength and geometric properties of new hybrids. The weathering integral to the material itself yields a painterly dimension over time. Materials that bear the marks of aging carry the messages of time.

Structural glass "U" planks during construction, Kiasma

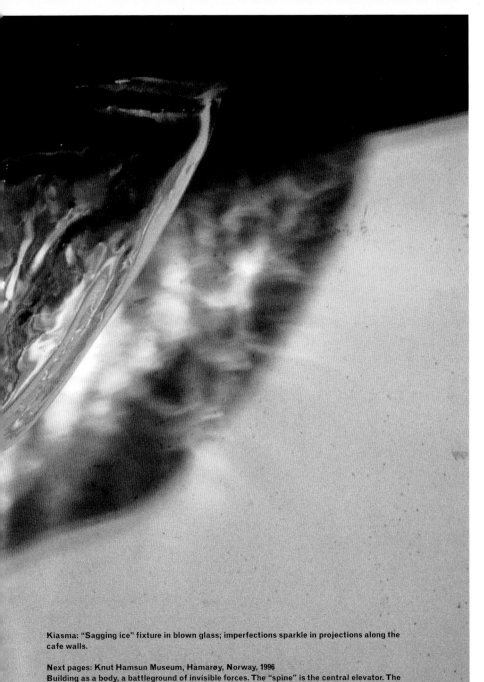

Kiasma: "Sagging ice" fixture in blown glass; imperfections sparkle in projections along the cafe walls.

Next pages: Knut Hamsun Museum, Hamarøy, Norway, 1996
Building as a body, a battleground of invisible forces. The "spine" is the central elevator. The structure is a tube of concrete covered with insulation and tarred black wood boards.

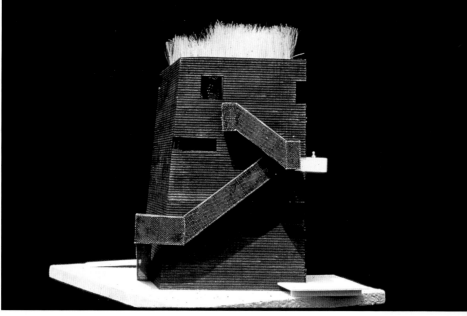

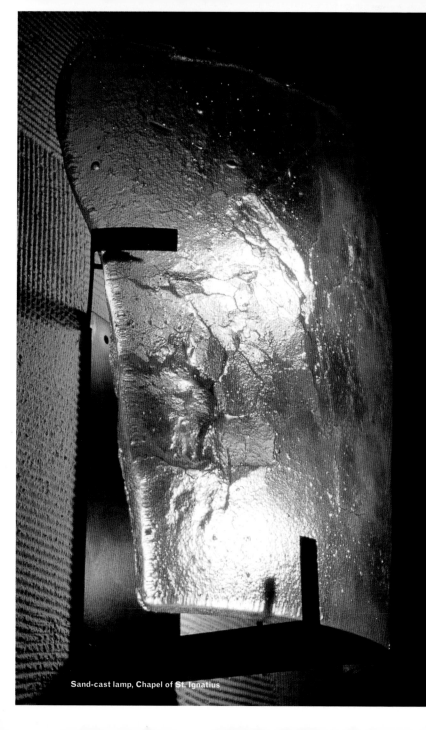
Sand-cast lamp, Chapel of St. Ignatius

Door pull, Martha's Vineyard House, 1987

We consider water a "phenomenal lens" with powers of reflection, spatial reversal, and the transformation of rays of light.

Liquid obeys the laws of gravity, yet in its lack of form it has phenomenal properties of rippling and reflection. The refraction of sunlight in liquid in a glass or the boundless horizon of the rolling ocean produces images that engage the psychological on at least two levels. The surface has texture, consistency, viscosity, and color. Inside there is a separate world, a miniature cosmos of organic and complex properties of molecular structure. Void of outer form, this inner world—like an inside longing for an outside— is an unstable but powerful stimulus.

We might consider water a "phenomenal lens" with the powers of reflection, spatial reversal, refraction, and transformation of rays of light. Colors and contours in the reflection of flowers or autumn trees in a clear still pond appear more intense than their actual view. A flat plate of glass in a window along an urban street reflects the background with an amazingly sharp image. On the bottom of a pool, we can often see intense focal lines of sunlight projected by the crests of wavelets that act as lenses. The psychological power of reflection transcends the "science" of refraction.

Below: Hailstone development, August 8, 1963, Weldon, Illinois

Right: Ripples of sunlight reflected in "Story of Water" Passage, Cranbrook Institute of Science

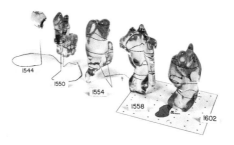

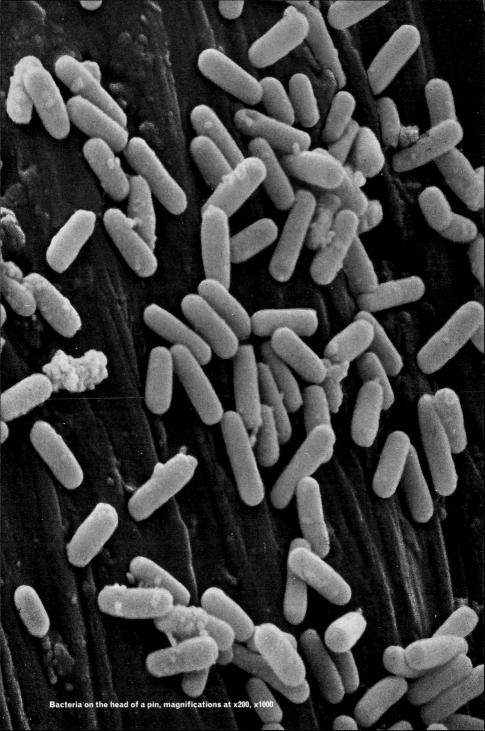
Bacteria on the head of a pin, magnifications at x200, x1000

Raindrops range in size according to their surface tension. From minute droplets of a mist to the fall, rotation, and coalescing of joined drops there is a natural range of size, a natural limit.

The Cranbrook Institute of Science's House of Vapor atomizes water drops—a haptic transformation of the material. Each drop is pressurized into 4000 droplets with a special nozzle. The droplets are so small that they do not condense on the glass walls of the room or on one's clothes when one enters. Technology stretches the capabilities of natural materials, transforming them. Materials are coerced into new natures.

Below: Detail, nozzle splits a drop of water into 4000 parts

Right: House of Vapor, Cranbrook Institute of Science

Next pages

Left: Study for house of ice

Right: Enyo Forest, California, oldest living things on Earth at 4900 years old. Bristlecone pines have been used to correct mistakes in carbon dating, that is, to correct mistakes in Western history.

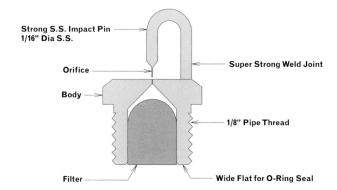

Strong S.S. Impact Pin
1/16" Dia S.S.

Orifice

Super Strong Weld Joint

Body

1/8" Pipe Thread

Filter

Wide Flat for O-Ring Seal

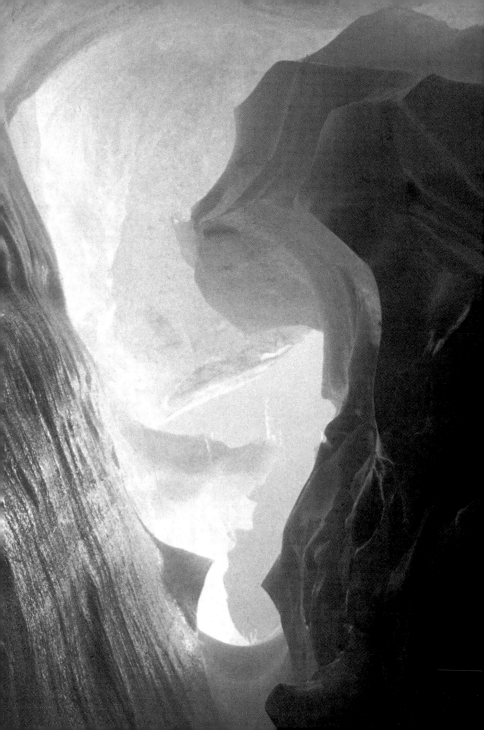

Oil-rubbed, carved Alaskan cedar doors

This page: Interlocking slabs and pick pocket plug

Right: 70,000 pounds in 21 tilt-up concrete slabs form the structural bearing walls of the Chapel of St. Ignatius

Similarly, new composite construction methods can create superstrong, lightweight shells (such as carbon fiber racing hulls). New fusing methods and new engineering technologies will reshape the haptic realm.

On a macro scale water is becoming more scarce, more precious. The limit of the global fresh water supply is already effecting urban change. The importance of water must be expressed at the micro and macro scale.

We are designing a new water treatment plant for the New Haven Regional Water Authority on a site beside Lake Whitney. The six-step process of the underground plant will be expressed in a six-quadrant park above. It is a new type of park dedicated to rejuvenating the habitat of diverse species. Water gardens in the park will be constantly replenished by the plant's runoff. We hope the diversity of insect, butterfly, frog, and other aquatic life forms will be studied by Yale students while the refuse of the plant, mud sludge, will be pressed into earth blocks, a material used for landscaping and retaining walls.

The term "dark matter" was conceived to describe what holds galaxies together. Galaxies spin so fast they should have spun apart ages ago. All their visible mass does not add up for the gravity required to hold them together. A new hypothesis describes "mirror matter" apparent only through its gravitational pull. Physicists speculate that mirror matter may be trapped in another dimension; its light stuck in a parallel universe, only its gravitational force is measurable. Dr. Lawrence Krauss, chairman of the physics department at Case Western Reserve, recently summarized, "Nature comes up with possibilities that no science fiction writer would dare suggest."

Lake Whitney Water Treatment Plant, New Haven, Connecticut, 1999; the six landscape sections correspond to the six treatment areas below the landscape.

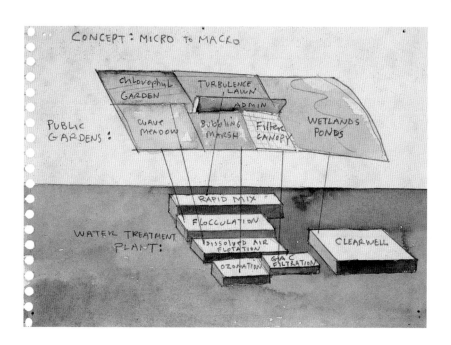

Concept diagram; the water treatment functions correspond to garden segments

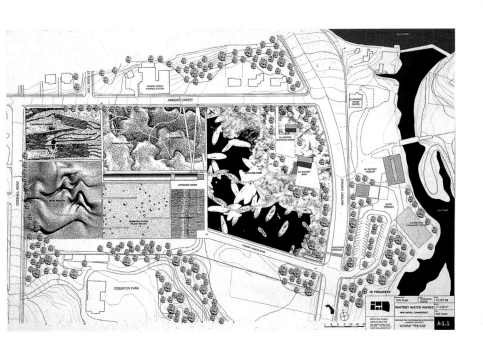

Concept plan: Each garden segment takes its morphology from an ultra-enlarged micro
biological form.

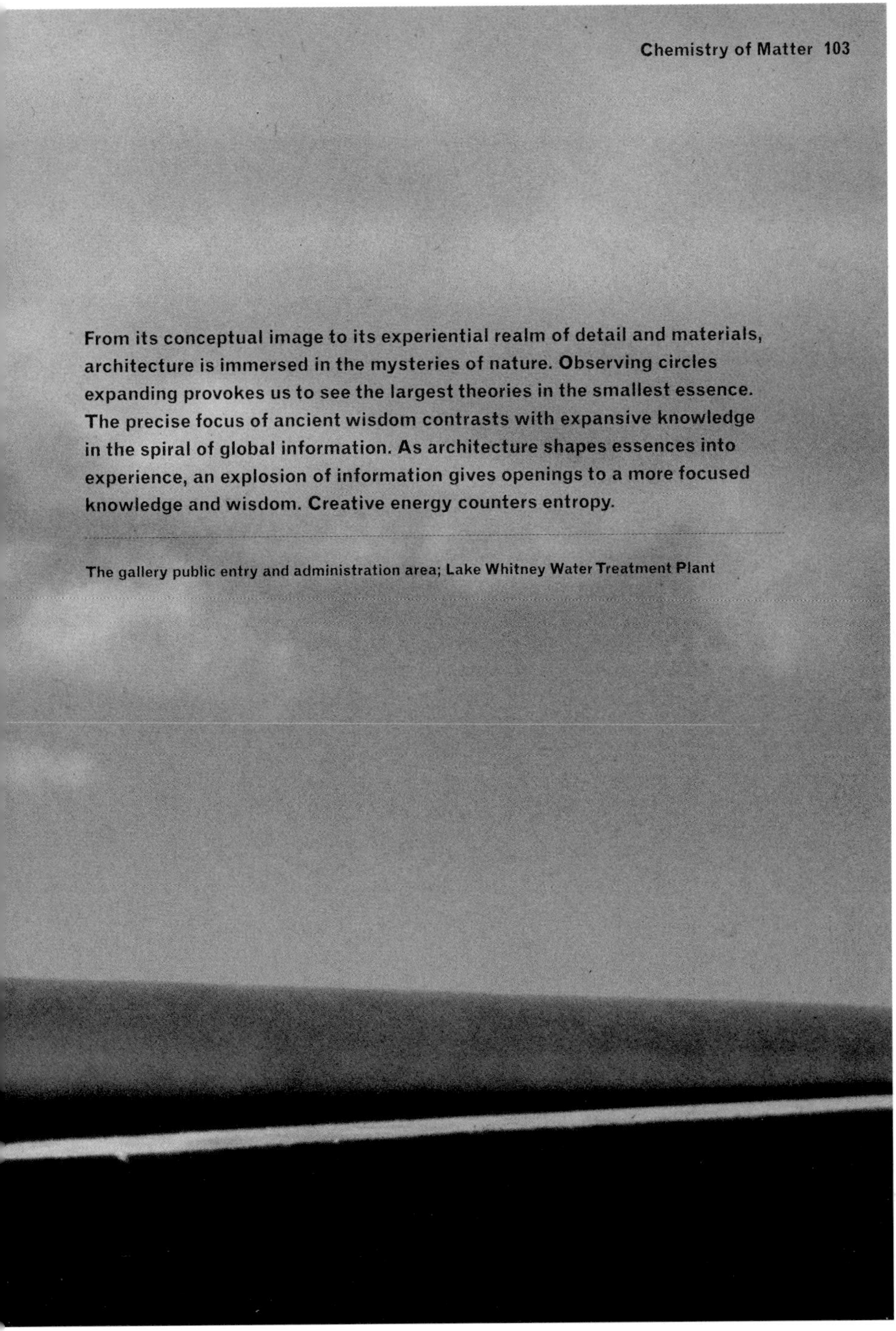

From its conceptual image to its experiential realm of detail and materials, architecture is immersed in the mysteries of nature. Observing circles expanding provokes us to see the largest theories in the smallest essence. The precise focus of ancient wisdom contrasts with expansive knowledge in the spiral of global information. As architecture shapes essences into experience, an explosion of information gives openings to a more focused knowledge and wisdom. Creative energy counters entropy.

The gallery public entry and administration area; Lake Whitney Water Treatment Plant

SPEED OF SHADOW
(PRESSURE OF LIGHT)

"There are some qualities, some incorporate things, that have a double
life which thus is made a type of that twin entity which springs from matter
and light."

—Edgar Allan Poe

Light can be read both as the phenomenon of light in words and the pressure
of light in science. Language without sentences, just like natural light, has
essences that transcend specific meanings and purposes. Language
becomes a form of light while light becomes language. Face to face with light
in a volume, luminous space becomes dreamlike. A moment of intense
sensibility ignites the intuition. Sideways, forward, backward...the empty
words of light are spoken in utter silence.

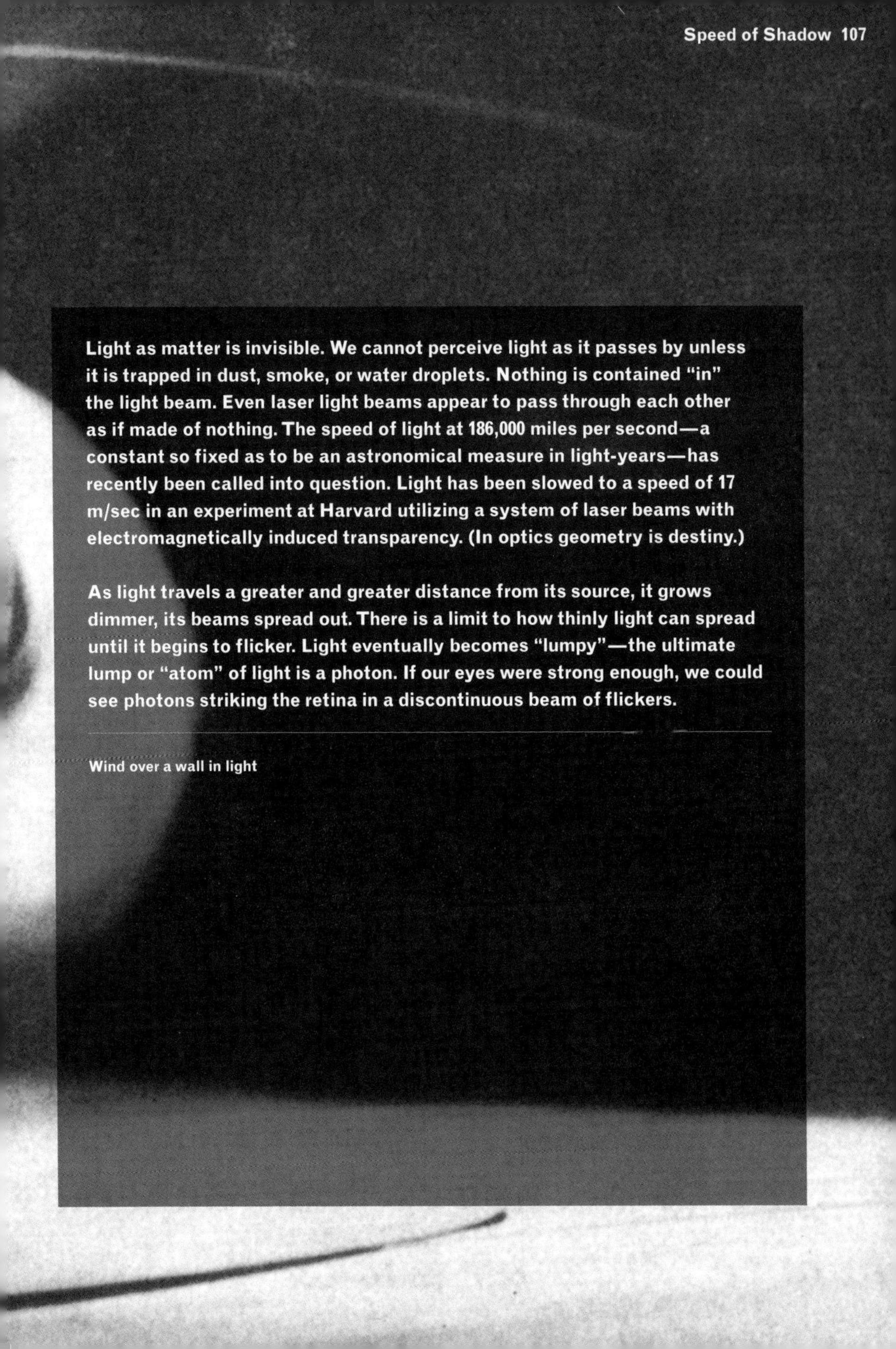

Light as matter is invisible. We cannot perceive light as it passes by unless it is trapped in dust, smoke, or water droplets. Nothing is contained "in" the light beam. Even laser light beams appear to pass through each other as if made of nothing. The speed of light at 186,000 miles per second—a constant so fixed as to be an astronomical measure in light-years—has recently been called into question. Light has been slowed to a speed of 17 m/sec in an experiment at Harvard utilizing a system of laser beams with electromagnetically induced transparency. (In optics geometry is destiny.)

As light travels a greater and greater distance from its source, it grows dimmer, its beams spread out. There is a limit to how thinly light can spread until it begins to flicker. Light eventually becomes "lumpy"—the ultimate lump or "atom" of light is a photon. If our eyes were strong enough, we could see photons striking the retina in a discontinuous beam of flickers.

Wind over a wall in light

As light passes through small holes it spreads out, frays, and bends. The resulting shadows do not necessarily look like silhouettes of the objects that cast them. Light bends in ways that yield shadows with bright bands, dark bands, or no sharp edges.

The physics of light is evident in shadows. The boundary between light and shadow—usually the gray area of "penumbra"—is filled with the mysteries of the mathematics of light. Is light a wave or a particle? Or does light characterize properties of both wave and particle simultaneously? Wave/particle duality connects us with the distant past.

Construction of Kiasma from the series "Unique in Architectural Time" by Solange Fabião

The presence of light is the most fundamental connecting force of the universe. At the time of the decoupling of light and matter the universe became transparent to light. For its first million years, current theory holds, the universe was opaque and shadowless.

Quantum theory forces us to accept the idea of parallel universes in terms of the photons and flickers of waves of light and shadows. The mysteries of the science of light approach the physiological delights of natural light in architecture: the faint glow of dim reflected daylight, the sheen of a plaster wall in a wash of sunlight, and the variations between heavy shadows and light shadows with reflected color. The range of astonishing phenomena of light and shadow contain mysterious ambiguities that glow elastically in a dreamlike uncertainty. A luminescence of shadow lines against a canvas or a sheet of white glass in the open air crystallize the theater of light. The infinite possibilities of light have been evident from the beginning of architecture and will continue into the future.

Light Laboratory, Cranbrook Institute of Science, 1998

The revelations of new spaces, like interwoven languages, dissolve and reappear in light. In magnificent spaces, light changes and appears to describe form. An eclipse of white clarity suddenly gives way to a pulse with color; light is contingent, its shadows intermittent.

Light that is not seen with the eyes can be felt. Light's psychological effects can lead to extremes of feeling with direct repercussions. Or we can speak of light in a dream.

In the Light Laboratory at the Cranbrook Institute of Science, every day is different. Low winter sun refracts in luminous waves while a prismatic rainbow washes the blank wall in unpredictable iridescence. Diffraction in gentle waves suddenly merges with pulsing shadows that appear as inverted dancers near the ceiling. The speed of shadow is vibrant.

The Light Laboratory, which is functionally the new entrance vestibule of the renovated institute, is an experimental construction employing new glass lens techniques patterning light in motion for a living architecture.

LIGHT SCORE

Properties of light also provide the organizing concept for the
Museum of the City we designed for Cassino, Italy. We attempted
to model the light on computers and quickly realized physical models
were necessary. In fact, light should be modeled full size as it falls
off a wall at the square of its distance to the source. The galleries
are organized in interlocking light sections. Between each section
is an interval, which is the equivalence of silence in music and which
forms a reversible sequence that can be "played" by bodily movement.
Each exhibition area begins as neutral space individuated through its
specific quality of light.

MUSEO CASSINO, KEY TO THE SCORE

c	curve-shaped light
l	linear light
cl	curved and linear light
cl.dr	curved and linear light with dropped ceiling
cl.md	curved and linear light with round slit
clS	curved and linear light with superimposed slides
rc	reversed corners
g	grabbed light
sqsq	two squares grabbing light
gg	double grabbed
ggS	double grabbed superimposed slides (to be superimposed)
gg?	double grabbed superimposed box
gg.dr	double grabbed with soffit
t.sq	center square cut out with tinted glass
oo.up	two round spaces stacked, upper view
oo.und	two round spaces stacked, under view
s	spiral space
/s	semi-circular space with slit on side
b	shell space (double s)
sqb	center square cut-out shell space
sqbS	center square cut-out and shell space superimposed slide
sq	center square cut-out
o	center round cut-out
orc	center round cut out and reversed corners
orcS	center round cut out and reversed corners superimposed sides
obx.und	round space stacked on a square space, under view
obx.up	round space stacked on a square space, upper view
öbx.und	round space with slit roof stacked on a square space, upper view

c

c
l   clS   cl

c
l   clS   cl
                            cl.dr

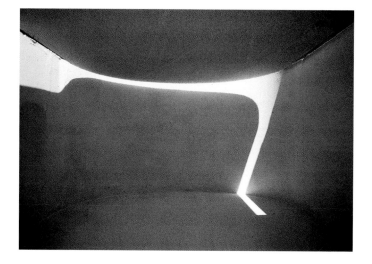

c

I clS

cl
cl.dr
cl.md

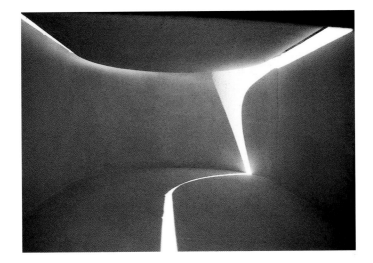

clS

cl

cl.dr

cl.md

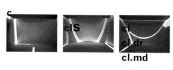

c

l clS

cl
cl.dr
cl.md

rc

c
l   clS

cl
cl.dr
cl.md

rc
g   sqsq

c
l   clS   cl
                cl.dr
                cl.md

                sqsq
                gg.dr

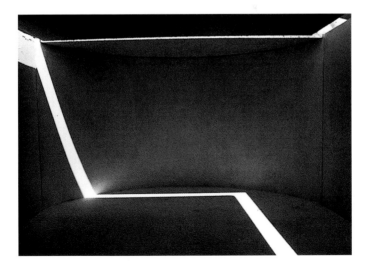

clS **cl**
cl.dr
cl.md

sqsq

gg.dr

  ggs **gg?**

c

   cIS

cl
cl.dr
cl.md

rc

g

sqsq
gg.dr

o   oo.up

gg

oo.und

ggs

gg?

c
l   clS   cl

cl.dr

cl.md

rc

g   sqsq

gg.dr

gg   ggs   gg?

o   oo.up   oo.und

c

l   clS   cl

cl.dr

cl.md

rc

g

sqsq

gg.dr

gg   ggs   gg?

o   oo.up   oo.und

t.sq

c

 clS   cl
                     cl.dr
   cl.md

rc
g   sqsq
                     gg.dr
    gg   ggs   gg?
         oo.up   oo.und
t.sq

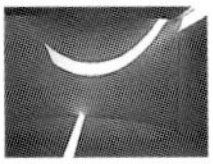

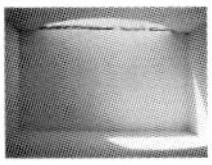

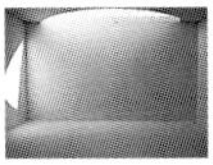

c

l   clS   cl
                                          cl.dr
                                          cl.md

rc
g   sqsq
                                          gg.dr
                                          gg   ggs   gg?

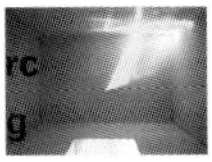

o   oo.up   oo.und

t.sq

t

clS   **cl**
             cl.dr
             cl.md

             sqsq
             gg.dr
             gg   **ggs**   **gg?**
o   **oo.up**   **oo.und**

t.sq

```
c
l              clS        cl
                          cl.dr
                          cl.md

rc
g                         sqsq
                          gg.dr
                          gg                      ggs        gg?
o              oo.up                   oo.und

t.sq
t

t
```

A space can be filled with the desire to "represent." If we can
imagine the mystery of how light feels, can we imagine its exact
natural, vocalized representation? And if we can characterize
a property of an interlocking light section, "L" is very valuable.
"G" and "S"are quite useful. The interval—which may be the
most important reflective space—is the all-so-important blank.
It begins to make sense as a score. We imagine that we can move
forward or backward in the spaces of light. A sense of theater
comes through as it holds in the rhythms of architecture's light.
In the absence of light, time functions as the difference between
relevance and irrelevance.

Rome is a city of shadows where light in the blaze of noon shows the motionless present. When I was a student at the University of Washington in 1969, considering a year of study in Rome, Professor Hermann Pundt handed me this quote by Goethe:

"Rome is a city where one could spend a lifetime in Pythagorean silence and still not know it."

In 1970 I moved to Rome. I lived behind the Pantheon at Via de Nari #6. I began each day with a visit to this magnificent space; each day the light and shadow were very different. The Pantheon is a great teacher, a laboratory of light with dynamic umbra.

When we were invited to submit an entry for Rome's Center for Contemporary Art competition in 1999, I felt the excitement of meditating on Rome again, beginning with the Arte Povera movement. The site for the competition—large steel north-light sheds once used as an automobile factory and then for the military—seemed appropriate for the center. Our urban concept for the hybrid of new and old connected the "trident" of the city plan with a twenty-four-hour through-block passage.

Building concept: Alternate circuits in three spectral lights

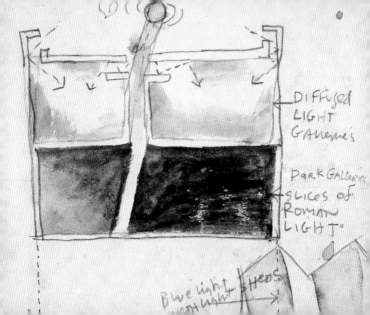

DIFFUSED
LIGHT
GALLERIES

DARK GALLERIES
SLICES OF
ROMAN
LIGHT.

Blue light
_____ light SHEDS

Above: Rome, 1999

Right, above: The site of the new Center for Contemporary Art connecting the Roman Trident

Right, below: Composite view of new building with existing sheds

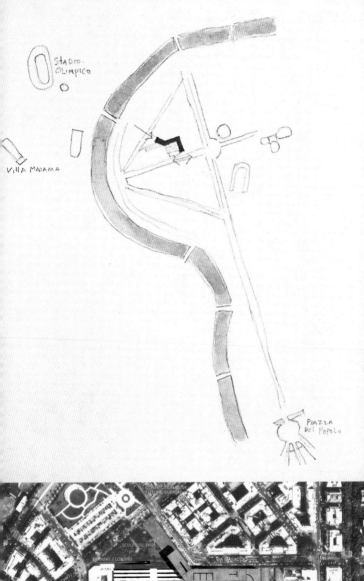

STADIO OLIMPICO

VILLA MADAMA

PIAZZA DEL POPOLO

CONNECTION WITH FUTURE SUBWAY

SCULPTURE PARK

PARKING / LOADING

VIA MASACCIO

VIALE PINTURICCHIO

VIA GUIDO RENI

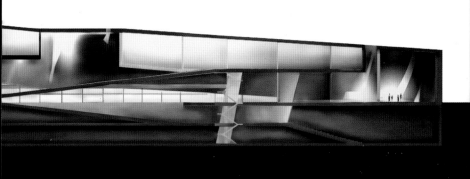

Unfolded section showing progression of light

Sequence of sketches through galleries with suspended gallery on left (light comes from below)

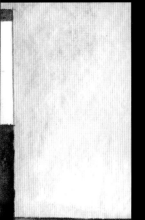

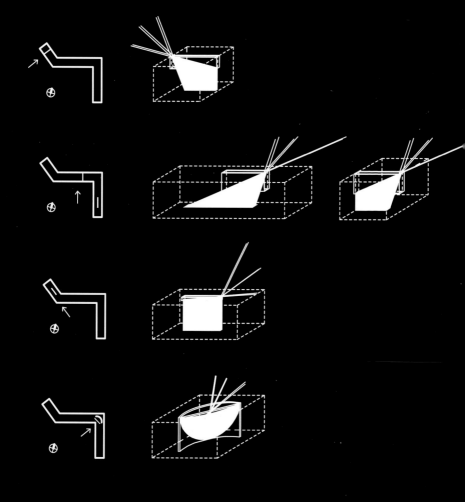

The building concept creates alternate circuits in three spectral lights: the existing sea of north-light sheds, the new diffused light galleries on the upper level, and the dark galleries with slices of Roman sunlight on the lower level. The south circuit begins in pure Roman light from above. The section gradually changes until one arrives at the north end, where the building is suspended and the light comes from below. The building was to be clad (as once was the Pantheon) in sheets of bronze. Light is bent by the force of gravity. In Rome, history bends light. The elephant struggles not just under the weight of the obelisk, but under the weight of history.

The twin entity of shadow and light allows us to read and understand the range of shadows—from the pure umbra of total shadow to the penumbra of extended sources of light, creating the reality in which we live. There is a "thingness" to light that one cannot form with one's hands. Light is not verbal; we need images, we need spaces. A new field of vision is opening to the pressure of light...the speed of shadow.

CHROMATIC SPACE

Color is a property of light. Yet physics does not hold the key to unlocking the enigma of colors, as the experiences of chromatic space are bound up in mystical effects and philosophical potential. Of course, we can describe color as simple radiation in nm (nanometer, one billionth of a meter). With this precision, 400–450 nm is violet, 450–480 nm is blue, 480–560 nm is green, 560–590 nm is yellow, 590–620 nm is orange, and 620–800 nm is red.

On a larger scale, radiation moves from radio wave to microwave, infrared, then visible light's little band, on to ultraviolet, X ray, and gamma ray. Traditional spectrographs could analyze only visible light. Today, advanced spectrographs open new worlds of information for cosmology. The recent discovery that the expansion of the universe is accelerating was made using red-shift measurements of visible wavelengths from receding stars. Astonishing advances in the physics of color may provoke us to rethink our everyday spatial experiences.

Below: Wavelengths, showing the narrow zone of visible light

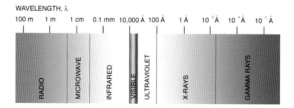

WAVELENGTH, λ

100 m   1 m   1 cm   0.1 mm   10,000 Å   100 Å   1 Å   10⁻²Å   10⁻⁴Å   10⁻⁶Å

RADIO   MICROWAVE   INFRARED   VISIBLE   ULTRAVIOLET   X-RAYS   GAMMA RAYS

NASA's *Far Ultraviolet Spectroscopic Explorer* (*FUSE*), a new spacecraft sending back its first observations, and the **X** ray observatory called *Chandra* are measuring deep-space phenomena. With these new tools, the universe is opening up to us. **X** rays and visible light are part of the web of electric and magnetic fields traveling through space. A perceptual phenomenon, in the context of chromatic space, is more than simply wavelengths.

Left: Green field, red lens

Below: The emission patterns from a star at rest ($z=0$) shift to longer wavelengths as the star recedes

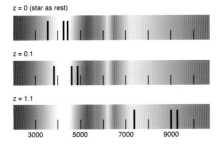

z = 0 (star as rest)

z = 0.1

z = 1.1

3000 5000 7000 9000

The urgent need of a thought-to-feeling bridge today is a main polemic of this book. Three hundred years ago scientific ideas, perceptual phenomena, and their aesthetic and mystical effects could be discussed together. For example Johannes Kepler's Mysterium Cosmographicum united art, science, and cosmology. Today, specialization segregates the fields; yawning gaps prohibit potential cross-fertilization. A scientist's world of statistics, cause and effect, and space-time—created with precise thought—is separate from the world of emotion and will. Thought and feeling should merge to provide a new catalyst for the imagination. The shadows of hard science could yield secrets far out into the unnavigated world. For architecture's inspirations every possible world at every scale must be explored. Eternities exist in the smallest detail.

In 1810, Johann Wolfgang von Goethe produced his "Theory of Colors." Goethe ignored wavelength. Instead, his work was aimed at perceptual relations and particular phenomena; it bridged a gap between the scientific and the phenomenological.

Below: Kepler's Mysterium Cosmographicum

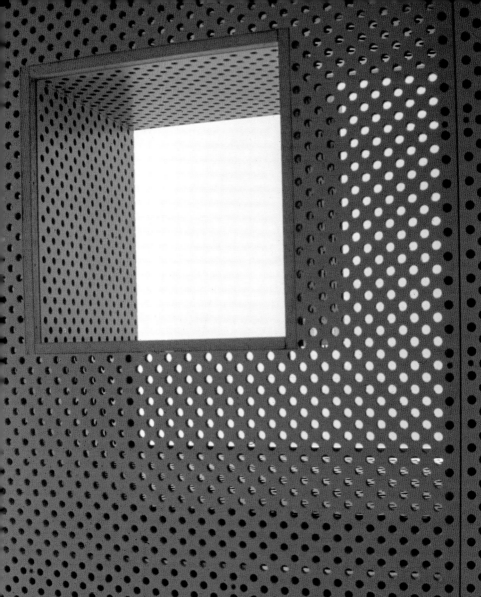

When passing clouds expose the sun, a phenomenal pulse of reflected color occurs.
Chromatic space is alive, like a breathing fluctuation.

Purple field, orange lens

Goethe's "Theory of Colors" addressed chromatic phenomena in space. He described the experience of fixing his eyes on bright flowers, then looking at a gravel path and seeing it studded with spots of the opposite color. The afterimage of marigolds is a vivid blue, while that of peonies is a beautiful green. This constant law of complementary color phenomena was observed acting on the whole retina. Goethe wrote, "If we look long through a blue pane of glass, everything afterwards appears in sunshine to the naked eye, even if the sky is gray and the scene colorless."

In a chapter on colored shadows, Goethe described blue shadows in snow, which gradually change to green due to the red color of the setting sunlight. An experiment to make colored shadows with a candle in moonlight yields double shadows: when cast by the moon and illuminated by the candle, a red-yellow shadow emerges; when cast by the candle and illuminated by the moon a beautiful blue appears. If these phenomena are too subtle for metropolitan life, then perhaps other moonless experiences will unfold on screens. The raw and vivid intensity as well as the subtlety of natural phenomena nevertheless retain a connective, almost biological force.

Ikebana in ice

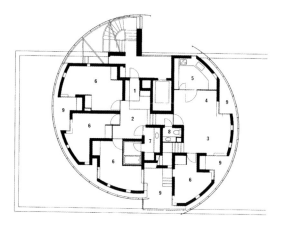

North Gate House Floor Plan
1. Entrance
2. Aisle
3. Living room
4. Dining room
5. Kitchen
6. Bedroom
7. Washroom
8. WC
9. Balcony

0 .5 1   2   3   5m
0 1 2 3 5   10   16ft

Ikebana House, Makuhari, Japan, 1996
A split cylinder with color on exterior and reflected color inside

In a small chapel we built for Seattle University in 1997, our concept of "a gathering of different lights" referred both to the large number of different backgrounds of the university's student body (60 nations represented) and to the liturgical division of the Jesuit university's chapel program. Seven bottles of light in a stone box organized the chromatic space of the architecture. Each "bottle of light" was made analogous to the dialectical of *The Spiritual Exercises* of Jesuit theory (question and answer). Fields of a complementary color in back-reflected, painted color planes are set against smaller colored lenses, creating a pulsing pair of opposites that shape the space. For a green field there is a red lens, for a blue field there is a yellow lens, for a yellow field there is a blue lens, for an orange field, a purple lens.

Bottles of light, Chapel of St. Ignatius, Seattle

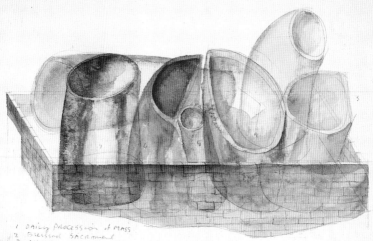

BARTHOLOMEW CHURCHES ... LIGHT
in a stone box

1 DAILY PROCESSION of MASS
2 BLESSED SACRAMENT
3 CHOIR
4 ALTAR
6 GATHERING   chapel of

Chapel of St. Ignatius

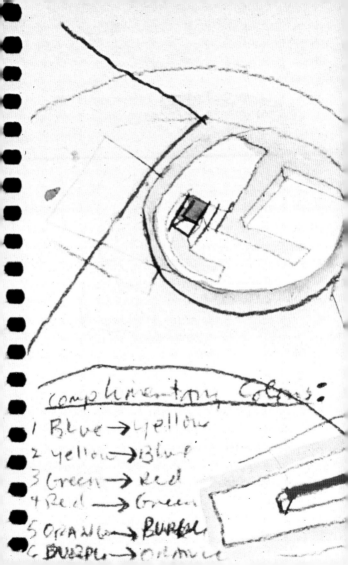

complimentary colous:

1 Blue → yellow
2 yellow → Blue
3 Green → Red
4 Red → Green
5 ORANGE → PURPLE
6 PURPLE → orange

Apse of ST IGNATIUS   10/20/94

"The appearance of the absolute in the form of the tangible." —Pierre Teilhard de Chardin, S.J.

The "thinking field" forecourt. Radiance of the inner space projected into campus space.

The creation of chromatic space was a central concept of the organization of two floors in the top of a Manhattan skyscraper in 1991 for D. E. Shaw, one of the world's first digital trading firms. Like the unseen work of the twenty-four-hour-per-day transactions, the unseen source of color from fluorescent, back-painted walls is projected by reflection of daylight and white fluorescent light. In chromatic space, light is phenomena, mystery, and wavelength.

Below: Concept diagram for D. E. Shaw Offices, New York, New York, 1992. Existing windows with new back-painted baffles.

Right: View from second level with reflected color

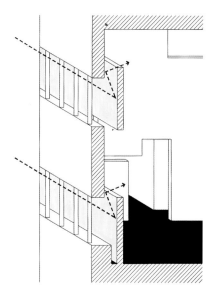

In Amsterdam, along the DeSingel Canal on Sarphatistraat, an experiment merging a "Menger sponge" with Morton Feldman's chance method used in "Patterns in a Chromatic Field" is under construction. In an office pavilion for the social housing company Het Oosten, the program is open and changing. Our ambition is to achieve a space of gossamer porosity with chance-located reflected color that "paints" the DeSingel Canal in reflection.

Due to the multiple layers of porous materials—from the perforated plywood and aluminum of the interior to the perforated copper of the exterior—light is bounced between the building's layers, forming a mutable "chromatic space" between the inner and outer layer. At night light will project in thick floating blocks of color.

Beyond the painted surfaces of a wall or a raw material's color, chromatic space is a dynamic spectral probe. Luminosity takes on volumetrics in moistened droplets suspended in midair. A forming blank glistens.

Left: Menger sponge

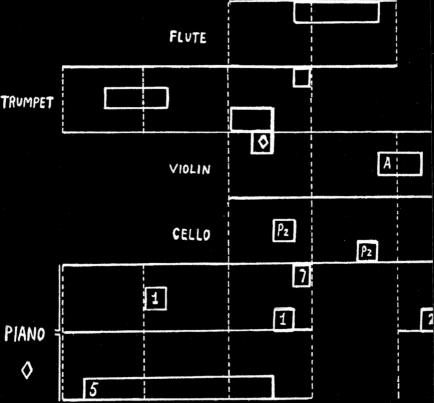

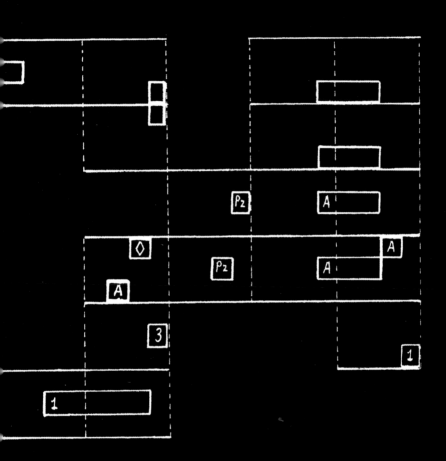

Sarphatistraat Offices, Amsterdam, Netherlands, 2000, interior view; modeled on a "Menger sponge," a single space where plan=section=elevation.

The pavilion merged Morton Feldman's "Patterns in a Chromatic Field" with a Menger sponge.

WORKING WITH DOUBT

"Convictions are more dangerous enemies of truth than lies." —Nietzsche

Absolute zero temperature, the hypothetical point at which a substance would have no molecular motion, is -459.72 degrees Fahrenheit. The "absolute zero" temperature in physics can be said to correspond to absolute music—music that has no program and does not try to tell a story or describe a scene. We have reached a marvelous moment in architecture in which determinant developments can occur from any discipline. Architecture, no longer limited to beginning in architecture, can be inspired by music, poetry, sculpture, or scientific phenomena—hundreds, thousands of beginnings. If an idea is realized, related to a specific site and circumstance, its differential combinations should connect to the organic nonlinear and the infinite.

An absolute exists in the specific. Site, geometry, program, circumstance, and materials are forged into spaces by an idea. A unique site and circumstance requires a specific idea, a "limited concept." More than just a verbally expressed idea, a limited concept sets a manifold relation. It refers to a nonhegemonic, local stability. It is semihierarchical. A limited concept states an ideal. An ideal aspiration in architecture is not eclectic. In the mind, an ideal is seen; it is a kind of perfection. It is closer to "classical" art than eclecticism. However, a limited concept thrives on going forward into the unknown, embracing doubt.

A concept can be in some cases mathematically precise. Mathematicians follow four laws in approaching a problem. They express it verbally, numerically, algebraically, and visually. Likewise architecture has a verbal concept, numeric size and proportion, algebraic integration of structure and material dynamics (and heat and cooling dynamics), and form. These four aspects forge an integrated connection for each site and program.

Mathematical codes dominate an absolute aim in today's Human Genome Project. They dominate the description of the double helix of DNA and yet James Watson and Francis Crick admit that a dream—the ultimate in subjectivity—was central to the discovery of DNA's structure. The subjective-objective transformations in the actions of life are not predetermined in genetic givens; we move, adopt, and live in new ways. In order to live and act we make errors, corrections, and correlations in an active advance; that is, we work with doubt.

The power of working with doubt or suspending disbelief is fundamental for creative thought in science and in architecture. Today the absolute is displaced by the relative and by the interactive. Instead of stable systems, we work with dynamic systems. Instead of simple and clear programs, we engage diverse and contingent programs. We work with, instead of precision and exactness, intermittent crossbred methods and combinative systems. The dynamic and interactive are qualities of contemporary architecture that set it apart from the clarity of the classic and the functional purity of the modern. Today we long for an absolute architecture after decades of ameliorating historicism. We desire an architecture that is integral rather than empirical, that has depth rather than breadth; we desire an architecture that will inspire the soul.

rking with doubt can yield an intrinsic affirmation of human choice that gives presence to an
a. Without intrinsicalness, there is no architecture. (Building construction continues regardless
the lack of architecture.) Architecture is for the bold in spirit; it rises to a pledge of inspired space
of a crowd of shrugging shoulders. A fusion of changing functions finds its flow within the open
ume of an emphatic testimony, so that architecture today can in and of itself shape and inspire
w feelings.

sterday's efforts to develop a technology for our needs have given way to an avalanche of new
hnologies and the challenge of incorporating them. Technology-guided function slips easily into
hnocratic architecture. Discoveries in science require a new relation to architecture, not a
ewal of monastic rationality or deterministic thinking. A nonconformist openness explores new
tentials while embracing archaic wisdom. Incongruous methods conduct explorations that are
tical of science and yet that utilize ultramodern techniques, creating supercharged doubt.

should aspire to build an architecture free of taking one thing for another. Rising like blood
a slapped face, architecture is not generic; its passion is set ricocheting through the generic,
using a positive chain reaction of embracing feeling. Architecture challenges the generic and,
an intense realization, forms become specific.

neralized, repeated, speculative constructions of rent-collecting maximization spring up
ntinuously across the continent. Indifference to quality of life is the norm. Banality in excess
lds a negativity, which has become apocalyptic in today's society. Faultless eyes watch social
rorism in the brittle world of suburban high schools. A fashionable (cynical) acceptance of
mmercial forces is opportunistic and unconvincing. Negative capability is the capacity to take
all that is problematic, and in the face of uncertainties, create. We need sincere architects with
gative capability and the imagination to forge a catalyst for change.

ther than a fixed and systematic background, a dynamic and relative world of change forces
placements. The hoped-for stable and unified theory in physics has given way to theories based
constantly changing parameters. Physicists speak of the universe as having a number of
ferent possible phases comparable to different phases of matter. Allowing different possibilities
architecture requires opening up thought, comparable to new science—working with doubt. To
ubt the validity of our ingrained opinions, ideals and views that we so hotly defend takes courage
d endurance. What is our central paradox? A joy in doubt in the deepest sense of being.

lowing: Absolute notation/indeterminate notation, first by John Cage, then by Cornelius Cardew, whose unfettered
roach embraced the radical openness of indeterminacy.

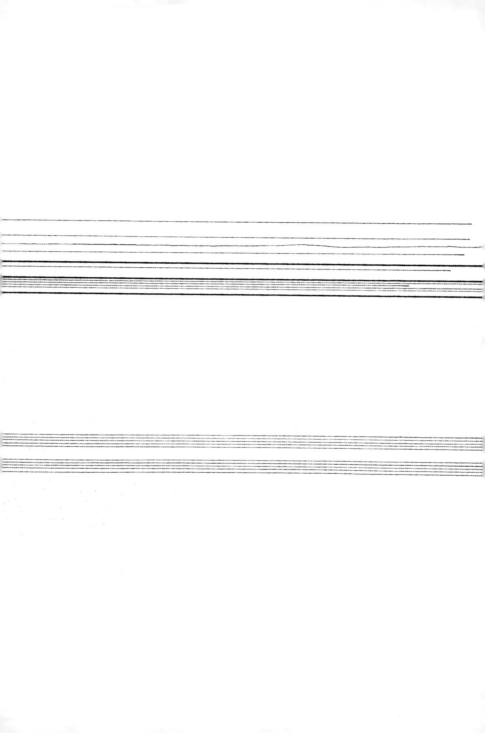

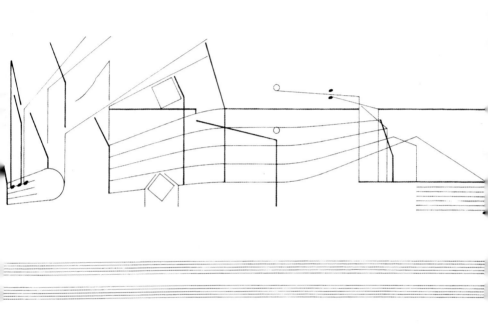

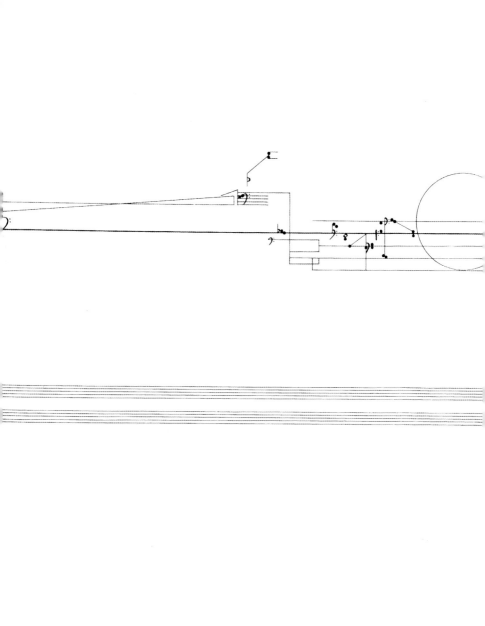

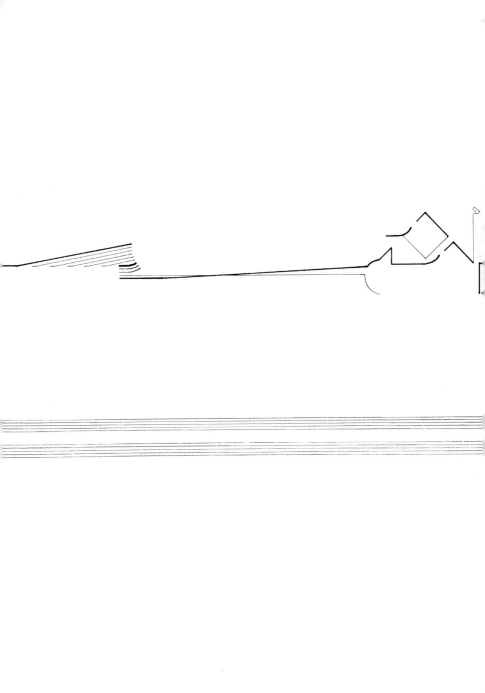

DURATION
(THE NOT YET MEETS THE ALREADY GONE)

"I simply think that water is the image of time, and every New Year's Eve, in some pagan fashion, I try to find myself near water... preferably an ocean... to watch the emergence of a new helping, a new cupful of time from it."

—Joseph Brodsky, *Watermark*

Henri Bergson argued in his book *Matter and Memory* (1911) that we cannot speak of time, we can only speak of duration. Duration, a fluid, flowing time, is intertwined with an experience of being where past, present, and future merge. If one extreme of time is the experiential time of individual being, the other extreme is the abstract, anonymous, measured time of science. As we strike a balance between these dynamic extremes, we are enmeshed in changing paradigms. Bergson's critique of chronometric theories of time argued for psychological time as duration—an argument in which time equals space.

Time/action diagram for Maya Deren's 1948 film *Meditation on Violence*. Two parabolic arcs describe three types of Chinese boxing in a single continuous movement. The last portion of the film is printed in reverse motion.

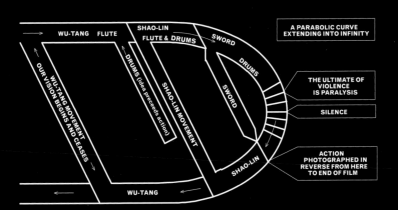

WU-TANG   FLUTE

SHAO-LIN
FLUTE & DRUMS

SWORD

DRUMS

SWORD

A PARABOLIC CURVE
EXTENDING INTO INFINITY

THE ULTIMATE OF
VIOLENCE
IS PARALYSIS

SILENCE

ACTION
PHOTOGRAPHED IN
REVERSE FROM HERE
TO END OF FILM

SHAO-LIN

WU-TANG MOVEMENT
OUR VISION BEGINS AND CEASES

DRUMS (idea precedes action)

SHAO-LIN MOVEMENT

WU-TANG

The theoretical conflict between absolute and relational views of space-time brings out very different concepts of identity, individuality, and property. Gottfried Wilhelm Leibniz argued for a relational point of view of time and space; this argument was crystallized by Albert Einstein's theory of general relativity. Still theoretical physics remains unresolved—our universe is evolving in time as our views are evolving. Time is only understood in relation to a process or a phenomenon. The duration of human beings alive in one time and place is a relational notion. The time of one's being is provisional; it is a circumstance with an adopted aim for the time being. Space—and architecture—exceeds the provisional.

Inspired by a first analysis of Bergson's *Matter and Memory*, in 1979 we designed and constructed a pool house and sculpture studio in Scarsdale, New York, based on a concept of "walls within walls." We attempted to engage time on several levels. First, the eighteenth-century stone wall of the site's perimeter became a point of departure in the cyclical and mythical time of the site. Second, the time of the day and the seasons were engaged in the angles of sunlight captured in the tiny project. Two large apertures in the longitudinal facades measured daily and monthly sun angle change, and two round windows punctured a corner to align with the summer solstice.

The construction of the pool house/sculpture garden presented us with an inspiring series of changing spatial perspectives upon approaching and circling the "walls within walls." Space was perceived by the body moving through time. This experiment was, for us, our first, crude space-time manifold.

"Walls within walls" concept diagram, 1979

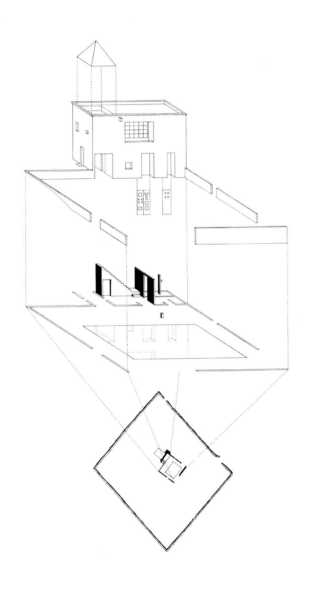

Walls within walls, Pool House and Sculpture Studio, Scarsdale, New York, 1979

Time—as experienced duration—is relative to an individual and to a space. Constantin Brancusi imagined and fabricated his own time capsule. His studio was an unchanging Carpation village in the middle of Paris with the *Endless Column* as its timepiece. Here, the finite time of place and culture was counterposed to infinity.

During our extensive work in Japan, with over sixty trips between 1989 and 1999, I became aware of another understanding of time. The concept of the fusion of space and time in "MA" are ancient and yet astonishing. Studying this concept opened my eyes to strange parallels in ancient Eastern and modern Western thinking. The Western argument that time persists merely as a consequence of the events taking place in it (time is nothing) is similar to the fourteenth-century monk Dogen's concept of "uji" or "being time." For the Buddhist, time is a continuous flux, a fluidity that makes every manifest form perishable and ontologically unreal. Existence and nonexistence are not different aspects of a thing—they are the thing.

Below: Diagram of sun angles, Makuhari Housing, Chiba, Japan, 1996. Each apartment must have four hours of sunlight every day.

Right: Constantin Brancusi's time capsule

Time in its various abstractions links architecture and cinema. Our design for the Palazzo Del Cinema competition for Venice (1990) involves three interpretations of time and light in space:

1. Collapsed and extended time within cinema is expressed in the warp and extended weave of the building. It is analogous to cinema's ability to compress time (twenty years into one minute) or extend it (four seconds into twenty minutes).
2. Diaphanous time is reflected in sunlight dropping through fissure space between the cinemas into the lagoon basin below. Ripples of water and reflected sunlight animate the grand public grotto.
3. Absolute time is measured in a projected beam of sunlight that moves across the "cubic pantheon" in the lobby.

A vessel for filmic time and filmic space, the building is bottle-shaped, with its mouth open to the lagoon towards Venice. The cinemas interlock within this frame, creating dynamic crevices and fissures that allow sunlight to reach the water below. In section, the cinemas turn slightly, like interlocking hands, changing their interior and exterior aspects of space.

Below: Concept diagram, Palazzo del Cinema, Venice, Italy, 1990
Right: Plan view of model

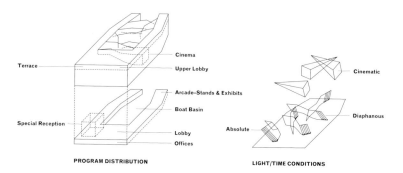

PROGRAM DISTRIBUTION

LIGHT/TIME CONDITIONS

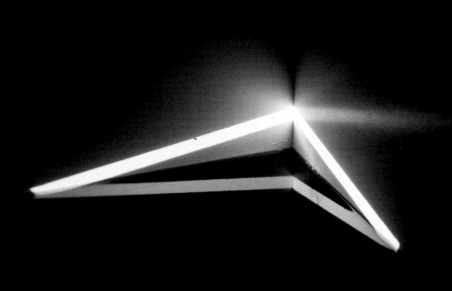

"Cubic pantheon," a space measuring seasons and hours

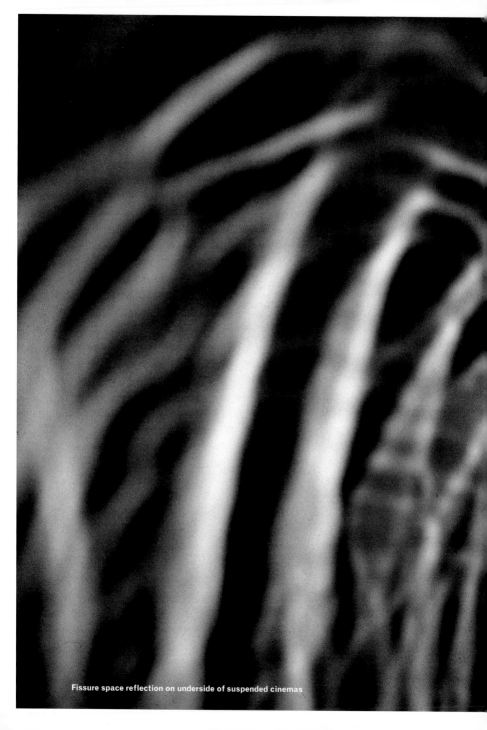

Fissure space reflection on underside of suspended cinemas

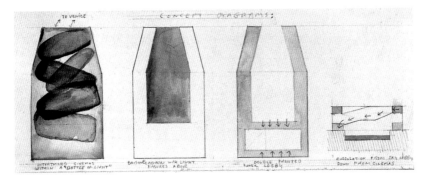

CONCEPT DIAGRAMS:

TO VENICE

INTERTWINED CINEMAS WITHIN A "BOTTLE OF LIGHT"

RAISING LAGOON WITH LIGHT FIGURES ABOVE

DOUBLE FRONTED LOWER LOBBY

CIRCULATION FROM SKY LOBBY DOWN FROM CINEMAS

Concept studies

Entrance from the lagoon

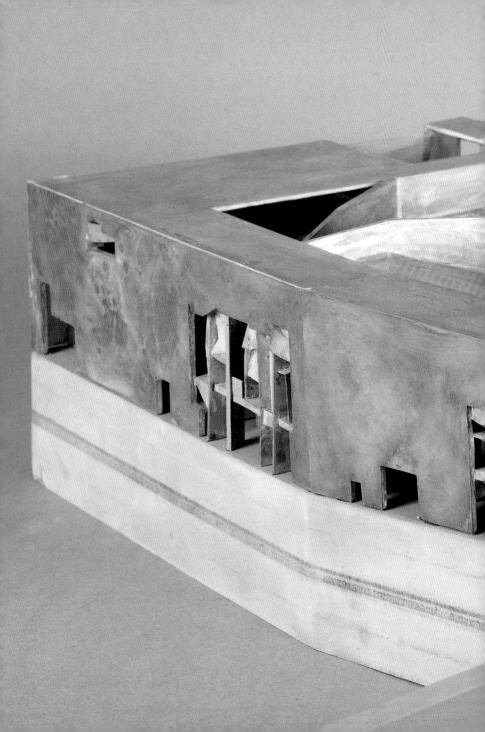

Study of filmic space provides a dynamic tool for the conception of architecture. In the beginning of Michelangelo Antonioni's *La Notte* for example, the camera pans down the surface of the Perelli Building in Milan, making a vertical parallax in urban space. Filmic space is often created in linking a series of interiors in sequence without an overall objectified exterior. Likewise an architecture can be created from the inside out.

Today, discussions of altering time's paradigms continue. Simultaneity and a new multiplicity of times are brought on by digital communication. Only with time's distance can a clear picture of these transformations emerge. In the end, all comparisons of time remain pertinent in a macrocosm in which space and time are only relations between our lived bodies and things that happen. Their experiential measure is duration.

below: Calendar of Epochs from ancient Mexico

Opposite: 256K dram microchip enlarged 4250x

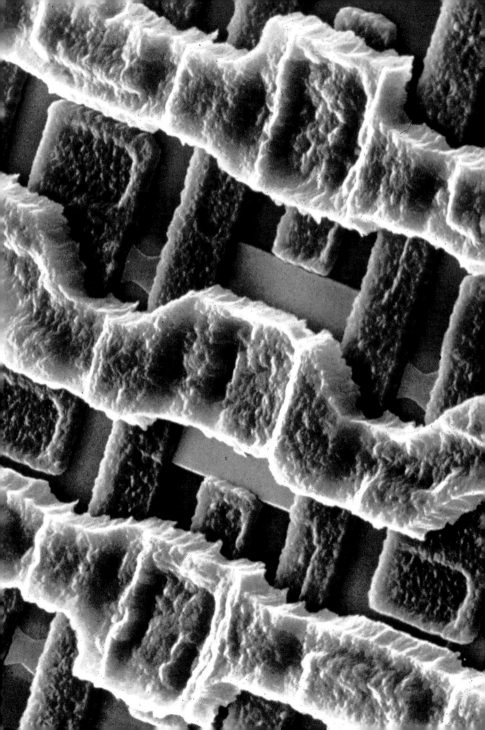

For Guadalajara, Mexico, as part of the initial phase of the new Cultural Center project, we designed a sector of 200 housing units and 150 hotel rooms divided into an Aerial (upper) Range and a Terrene (lower) Range. The interlocking sections offer each apartment and hotel room north and south views. The Aerial Range hovers twenty meters above the ground of a former cornfield. It is extroverted toward distant views, while the Terrene Range is introspective, focusing toward garden courts. The ranges contain a hybrid of hotel and housing with garden hotel rooms along the north of the Terrene Range and permanent apartments in the Aerial Range. Silent Interval Plazas are cut through the mat of the Terrene Range using the geometry of the shadows from the Aerial Range.

Two spatial horizons suggest two time horizons. The ancient Mexican calendar has eighteen months of twenty days each. There are eighteen arms in the Aerial Range. The five "interval spaces" carved from the Terrene Range correspond to the ancient Mexican epochs. Each of these spaces provides the entrance for twenty houses.

Due to the "glyphtic section" the sun's shadows mark present and future via a numeric connection to ancient time. Architecture aspires to the infinite and yet a project can become "pure dissipation." Without respect to before or after, beginning or end, cause or effect, the not yet meets the already gone.

Left above: Guadalajara Housing & Hotel, Guadalajara, Mexico, 1998. Hanging walkways give access to upper stratum.

Left below: Upper stratum slides public spaces into lower stratum

Below: Glyphic diagram: shadows cut public squares in housing mat

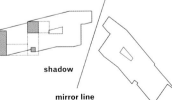

March 21st, 3 P.M.

shadow

mirror line

Site plan: An existing cornfield to be a new town

Concept diagram: Domestic space of shadow and light

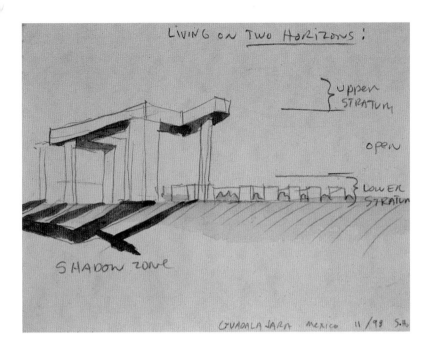

LiViNG on Two HoRiZonS !

} upper STRATUM

open

} LoWER STRATUM

SHADow zone

GUADALAJARA mexico 11/98 S.H.

Concept diagram: Housing and hotel mixed in two horizons

Upper stratum with suspended walkway access to rooms

CORRELATIONAL PROGRAMMING

Modern life is characterized by programmatic fluctuation: turbulent shifts
in demographics, changes in the desires of restless populations, and the
alternation of local and regional political wings. The initial program brief
of even a single building is typically shaken up and reorganized during
the planning process. When a portion of the program is taken away, new
programs are invented to occupy the building envelope.

The disquietude of programmatic fluctuation can be taken as an advantage.
Is programmatic indeterminacy a disaster for any architect who aspires to
a relationship of form to function? Will the profusion of the articulated-skin
approach prevail simply as a solution for internal indeterminacy?

Chi-Chi has a bath against her will.

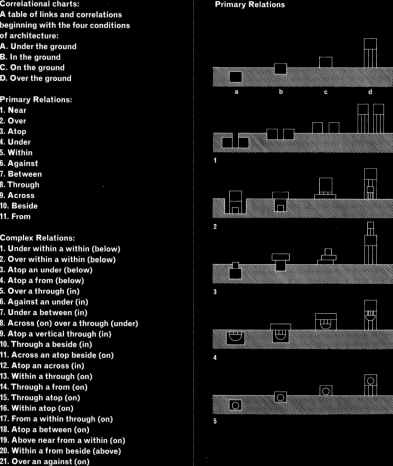

Correlational charts:
A table of links and correlations
beginning with the four conditions
of architecture:

A. Under the ground
B. In the ground
C. On the ground
D. Over the ground

Primary Relations:

1. Near
2. Over
3. Atop
4. Under
5. Within
6. Against
7. Between
8. Through
9. Across
10. Beside
11. From

Complex Relations:

1. Under within a within (below)
2. Over within a within (below)
3. Atop an under (below)
4. Atop a from (below)
5. Over a through (in)
6. Against an under (in)
7. Under a between (in)
8. Across (on) over a through (under)
9. Atop a vertical through (in)
10. Through a beside (in)
11. Across an atop beside (on)
12. Atop an across (in)
13. Within a through (on)
14. Through a from (on)
15. Through atop (on)
16. Within atop (on)
17. From a within through (on)
18. Atop a between (on)
19. Above near from a within (on)
20. Within a from beside (above)
21. Over an against (on)

Primary Relations

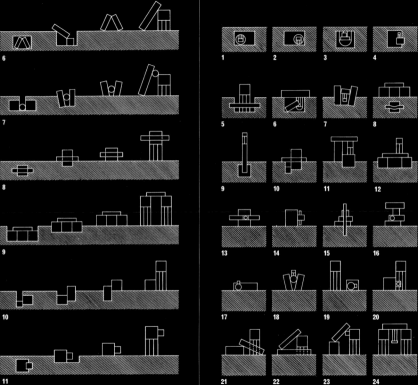

The micro program of a student's dormitory room, MIT

Criss-crossing clogged

Let the architect fill spaces and buildings with a conscious programmatic richness. The restrictions of internal functions in a large project unfurl against an open thought process of programmatic association. Spatial sketches can be opened to program suggestions (action images gathered and juxtaposed).

We are not calling for a new disordered architecture to match the disorder of culture; this would only affirm the chaotic. Rather, we propose experiments in search of new orders, projections of new relationships. We do not wish to transpose our study into a system or method. The energy inherent in opening up relationships presents us with a continuity of ordering that compels reflection.

Consider the experience of reading a morning newspaper. Here is an ordering of untenable juxtapositions that could be paralleled in urban and architectural terms: beside an article describing a billion-ton floating island of ice that supports twelve research buildings drifting around the North Pole is an item on the construction of a twenty-four-foot diameter aqueduct, and a piece on the austerity program of a religious cult. Next to a column on insomnia and the sleep movement of plants is a huge diagram of the Pacific Rim trade network, an article on Japanese factories in Mexico, and a photograph of a hole in the ozone layer over the South Pole. To precisely translate thoughts and feelings sparked by incredulous relationships is as problematic as translating an English word into all of the world's 2796 languages. Rational precision gives way to intuition; subjective dimensions ground physical dimensions.

Porta Vittoria, Milan, Italy, 1986

Makuhari Housing: Activist buildings between and on silent buildings

Top: Early model of West Gate House

Bottom: Correlational chart showing urban relation of figure and ground

Right: North Court House

Isolated buildings with a single function are scarce in the city. The abutment and connection of buildings causes functions to intersect. Various urban building relationships suggest corresponding programs.

Correlational programming questions, compares, and contemplates diverse combinations without absolute claims to instrumentality. Its purpose is to make one think, and to occupy space in new ways.

A spatial arrangement, a smell, and a musical phrase may be imagined simultaneously. A visual field can provoke subject matter and imply programs to an imaginative perceiver. We could speak of the sounds implied by an array of brittle linear forms, or the way a view smells. An individual's experience can be limited by cultural associations, recognition of materials and imagination of their properties, and the physiological effects of space and enclosure. But the perceiver's angle of vision and preconception is potentially open to limitless associations. Rather than allow prejudice to be a primary subjective determinant of design, one could induce program associations by increasing the possible number of programs to occupy an urban setting.

Silent, heavy-frame buildings and lightweight, activist structures

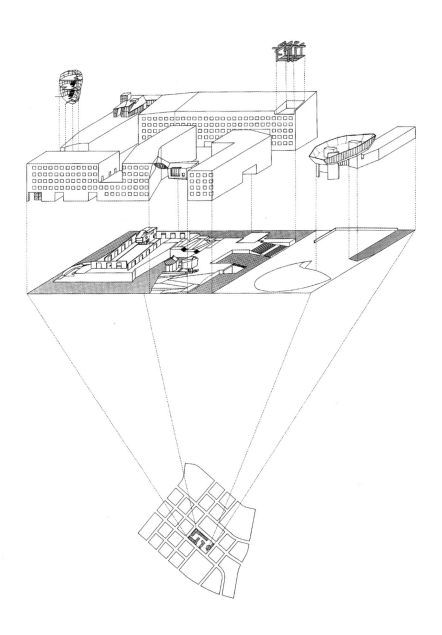

Above: View toward South Court House

Right: East Gate House with Ikebana House in distance

HINGED SPACE
(FROM AUTONOMOUS TO INTERACTIVE)

Beyond autonomous, room-by-room space is interactive space, where "participating walls" reorder domestic environments. Adjustable space comes alive, especially in the domestic spaces of Manhattan or Tokyo, where every square meter is a universe. Unlike the cumbersome "moveable partition" systems of the 1960s, participating walls are a hybrid of fixed and hinged walls. Space becomes dynamic and contingent.

Time-lapsed view showing natural rotation of Earth around fixed point of North Star

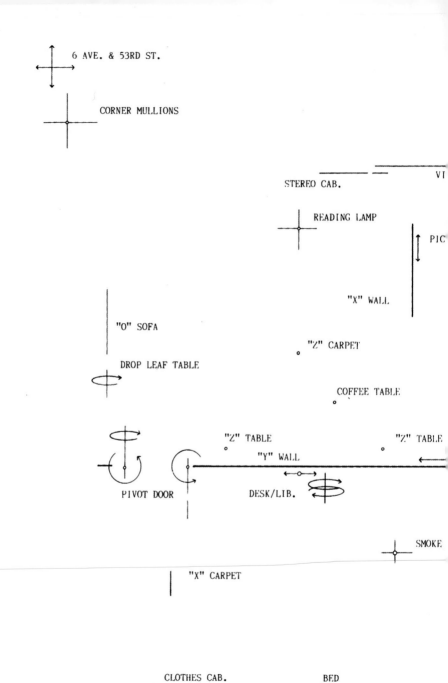

6 AVE. & 53RD ST.

CORNER MULLIONS

STEREO CAB.

VI

READING LAMP

PIC

"X" WALL

"O" SOFA

"Z" CARPET

DROP LEAF TABLE

COFFEE TABLE

"Z" TABLE

"Z" TABLE

"Y" WALL

PIVOT DOOR

DESK/LIB.

SMOKE

"X" CARPET

CLOTHES CAB.

BED

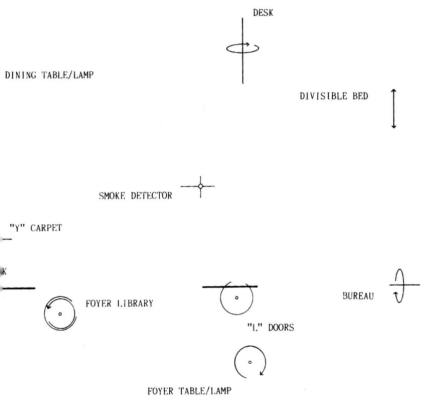

DESK

DINING TABLE/LAMP

DIVISIBLE BED

SMOKE DETECTOR

"Y" CARPET

K

FOYER LIBRARY

"L" DOORS

BUREAU

FOYER TABLE/LAMP

XYZ Apartment, MoMA Tower, New York, New York, 1985

In 1983, we began to experiment with hinged space in a series of apartment designs in Manhattan (the Cohen Apartment, the XYZ apartment at MoMA Tower, and the Theological Apartment). The then-current polemics of "deconstruction" led other designers to create twisted grids, shards of walls, and tortured folds. When their geometries were built, space was frozen into a caricature of the dynamic. Our three apartments attempted to create a space of movement and dynamism promised by the current trends in deconstruction. Rather than moving geometries that were static in realization, these geometries moved altering experiences of space, changed in parallax.

XYZ Apartment rotational wall

In Fukuoka, Japan, we realized twenty-eight apartments with hinged space. Each of the apartments is different and interlocks like a Chinese puzzle around four "void" water courts. The hinged-space dynamic allows an interactive reformation of the entire domestic space. The apartment spaces are organized in several hinged-space types. In some cases, entire room corners pull away with rotating walls. Domestic life changes with the space in diurnal, perennial, and episodic cycles.

Void Space/Hinged Space Housing, Fukuoka, Japan, 1991

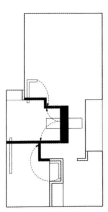
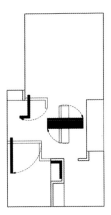

In 1994, I collaborated with Vito Acconci on the design of the facade for the StoreFront for Art and Architecture in Manhattan. The interactive dynamic of the gallery argued for an inside-out facade, which addresses insular art and turns it out to the public street. Hinged walls rotate on both axes, which allows some to become tables and benches. The body is linked to the wall forms in the crude way that the shoulder is needed to push space out or pull it in.

Rather than pure, minimal space, this space is crossbred. It can be exact and then suddenly change into dynamic combinative space. It can be severe or easygoing. When the facade is closed, it takes the typological form of a Manhattan, triangular slice of shop front. When it is open, it becomes drawn into the city outside. The three-dimensional volume can be disposed towards the four dimensional with changes in time. With this facade StoreFront realized a new type of dynamic, urban, and interactive space, even though the entire budget of this project equaled that of one custom carpet for a luxury apartment!

StoreFront for Art and Architecture, New York, New York, 1994

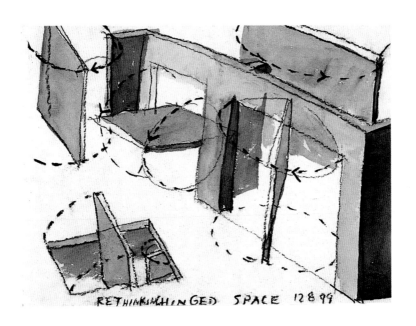

RETHINKINGHINGED SPACE 12899

Closed StoreFront

Partially open StoreFront

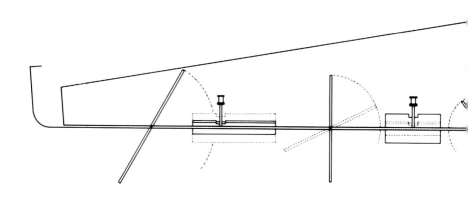

StoreFront hinged space: Facade turns inside out.

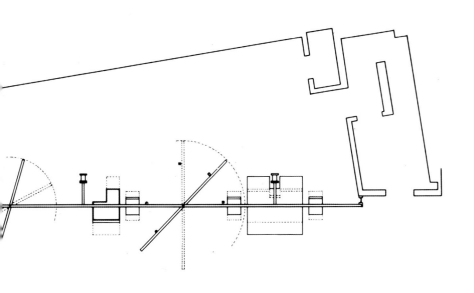

At night, hinged space walls become projection screens for some exhibitions.

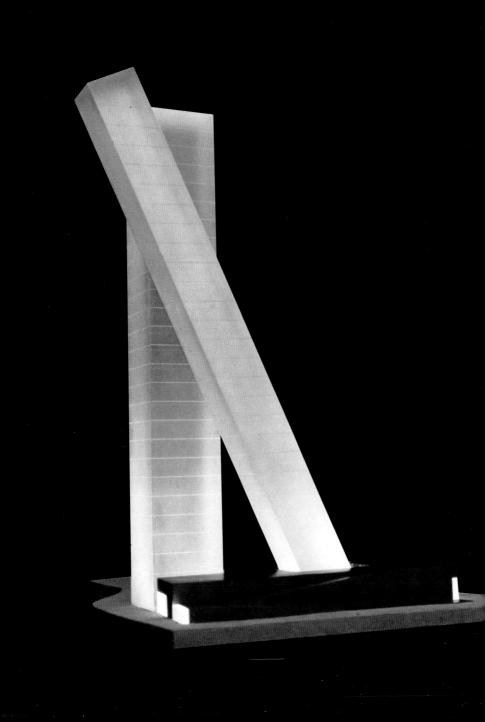

The tilt of the Earth's axis at 23.5 degrees became the heuristic device shaping the geometry for our design of a town center tower in Vuosaari, Finland. Vuosaari—near Helsinki, the most northern metropolis on Earth—is a place where the view to the northern end of the Earth's axis always points to the North Star.

From Vuosaari's Central Station, the tower frames a view to the sea over a public plaza. The dwellings in the new "x" towers aim at flexibility, change, and functionality. Hinged-space doors in various rotations allow many combinations of private and public rooms. On floors ten through twenty-five the towers join, allowing large hinged-space apartments to connect between the buildings. The nighttime view of the new town center presents a glowing presence, a gateway to the Baltic, in this place of bipolar rotation.

Left: Town Center Tower, Vuosaari, Finland, 1999

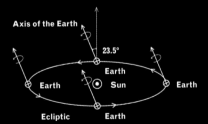

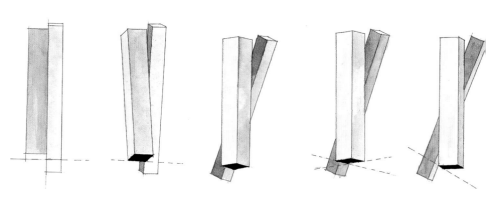

Rotation around the gateway tower: A new orientation device in the city

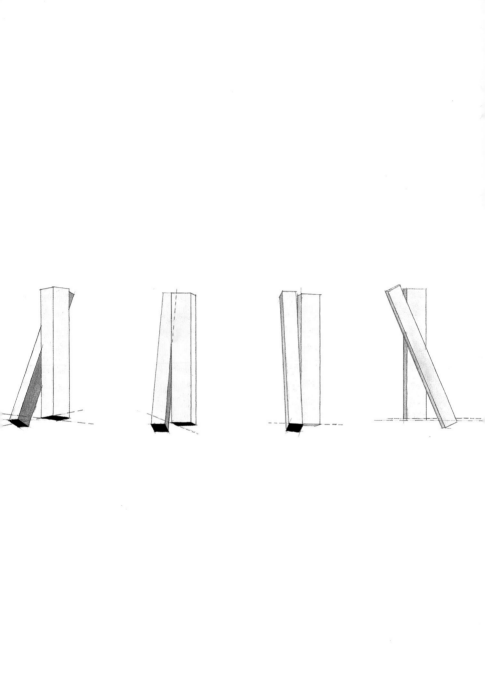

Interior of apartment connecting two towers

Above: Night view with gateway to the town center

Right: Plans ascending

THE STONE AND THE FEATHER
(LANDSCAPE INTO ARCHITECTURE)

"Whole thing works on gravity. Heavy falls and the light floats away."

—Wheat rancher explaining how a threshing machine operates

Buckminster Fuller was a pioneer of the lightweight, of liberating the building from gravity. He invented a conscious lightness. "How much does your building weigh?" was his question. He counterpoised heavy stone, brick, and timber with the birdlike frame and the featherweight tensile skin. His systems of spider-web tensile domes and frames rejected the heavy for the light, linking weight and efficiency to politics and power.

In contrast to Fuller's singular, monistic philosophy, Italo Calvino's musings in one of his last texts, *Six Memos for the Next Millennium*, stated that "two opposite tendencies have competed in literature: one tries to make language into a weightless element that hovers above things like a cloud, or perhaps the finest dust, or better still a field of magnetic impulses. The other tries to give language the weight, density, and concreteness of things, bodies, and sensations." (Cambridge, MA: Harvard University Press, 1988, p.15) Calvino circumscribes weight and weightlessness as two separate conditions.

A phenomenal architecture calls for both the stone and the feather. Sensed mass and perceived gravity directly affect our perceptions of architecture. The weight of the low, thick, brick arches in Sigurd Lewerentz's Church at Klippan outside of Stockholm conveys the power of gravity and mass. Dim light gains its power from both the heaviness of the brick masses overhead and its effect on the inner spaces. A duality exists in the bricks' weight pressing in on the dim light.

Fuller tensile experiment from the book *Inventions*

$$\frac{\text{material x sound}}{\text{time}} = \frac{\text{material x light}}{\text{space}}$$

Architecture's expression of mass and materials according to gravity, weight, bearing, tension, and torsion reveal themselves like the orchestration of musical instruments. Material is made more dynamic through the contrast of heavy (bass, drums, tuba) and light (flute, violin, clarinet). The contrast in mass of the bass instruments in Béla Bartok's "Music for Strings, Percussion, and Celeste" is emphasized by the physical separation of the light and heavy instruments on stage during the performance of the piece. The materiality of music is resonantly conveyed via the instruments to aural temporal experience. A heavy and light materiality is likewise conveyed via the structure, material, and spatial experience of architecture.

The Stretto House we built in Dallas, Texas, in 1991 was an experiment in parallel to the Bartok composition. The composition in four movements alternates from the heavy "spatial dams" of concrete block to the billowing, tube-framed, lightweight roof structures. The house flows like the adjacent stream as it merges with the landscape laterally. The center of the composition is a "flooded room" where the waterscape fuses with the building. The heavy and light tectonic concept aims toward a new field of landscape merging with architecture.

Below a: Failure of steel in tension, by shearing at 45 degrees and by necking

Below b: Compression failure in wood

Left: Stretto House, Dallas, Texas, 1991

a | b

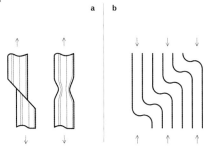

The force of gravity as a function of mass and distance can be expressed by $F=GmM/r^2$. On the moon with less gravity, objects have less weight. Gravity draws a stone quickly to the ground, while a feather zigzags slowly through the air, lifted by the opposing forces of friction and buoyancy.

The ideal of complementary contrast drove our design for an addition to the 1933 Nelson-Atkins Museum in Kansas City, Missouri, a model of classical stone temple and surrounding landscape. We envision a new paradigm fusing landscape and architecture in the new portion of the museum. In contrast the new lightweight architecture of glass lenses is scattered about the landscape, engaging the great sculpture garden. The visitor's experience will be newly charged with an experience of views and partial views of landscape; sequences of shifting perspectives charge spaces where landscape merges with architecture.

Right: Diagram from Rosalind Krauss's argument "Sculpture in the Expanded Field"

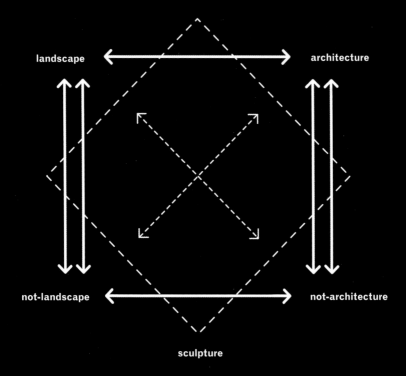

landscape   architecture

not-landscape   not-architecture

sculpture

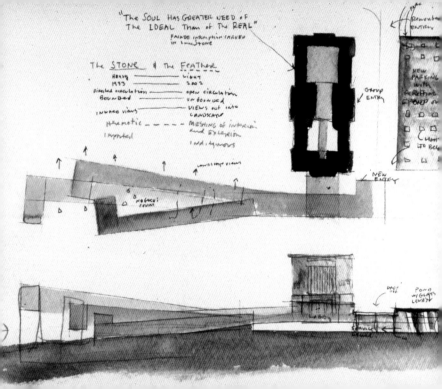

"THE SOUL HAS GREATER NEED OF
THE IDEAL THAN OF THE REAL"
FACADE INSCRIPTION CARVED
IN LIMESTONE

THE STONE & THE FEATHER

HEAVY	LIGHT
1933	2002
DIRECTED CIRCULATION	OPEN CIRCULATION
BOUNDED	UNBOUNDED
INWARD VIEWS	VIEWS OUT INTO LANDSCAPE
HERMETIC - - - -	MESHING OF INTERIOR AND EXTERIOR
IMPORTED	INDIGENOUS

GROUP
ENTRY

NEW
ENTRY

PEDESTRIAN
ENTRY

NEW
PARKING
WITH
BREATHING
SPACED OF

LIGHT
LTD BG

LANDSCAPE VIEWS

NOGUCHI
ROOM

POND
W/ GLASS
LEVEL

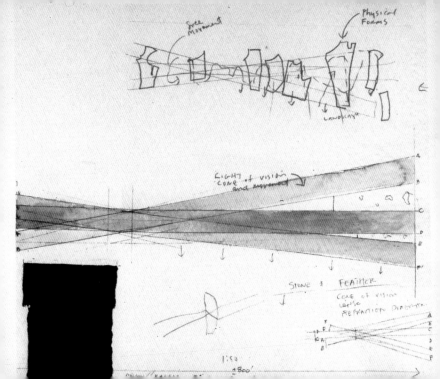

EYE Movement

PHYSICAL FORMS

LANDSCAPE

LIGHT of vision
cone and movement

STONE & FEATHER
CONE of vision
LENSE
REFRACTION DIAGRAM

1:50
+800'

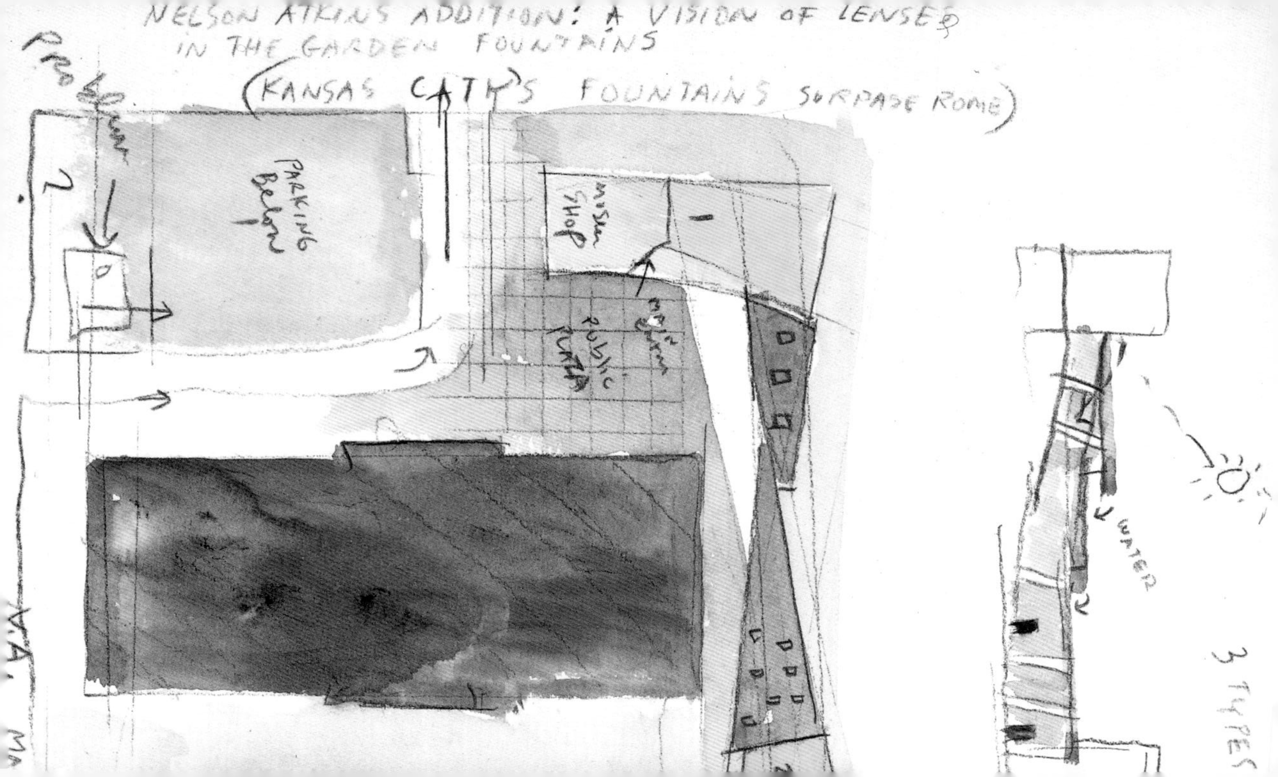

3 TYPES

↓ WATER

NELSON ATKINS ADDITION: A VISION OF LENSES
IN THE GARDEN FOUNTAINS
(KANSAS CITY'S FOUNTAINS SURPASS ROME)

main entry

mosin
SHOP

Public
PLAZA

PARKING
Below

PROBLEM

?

V.A.   MA

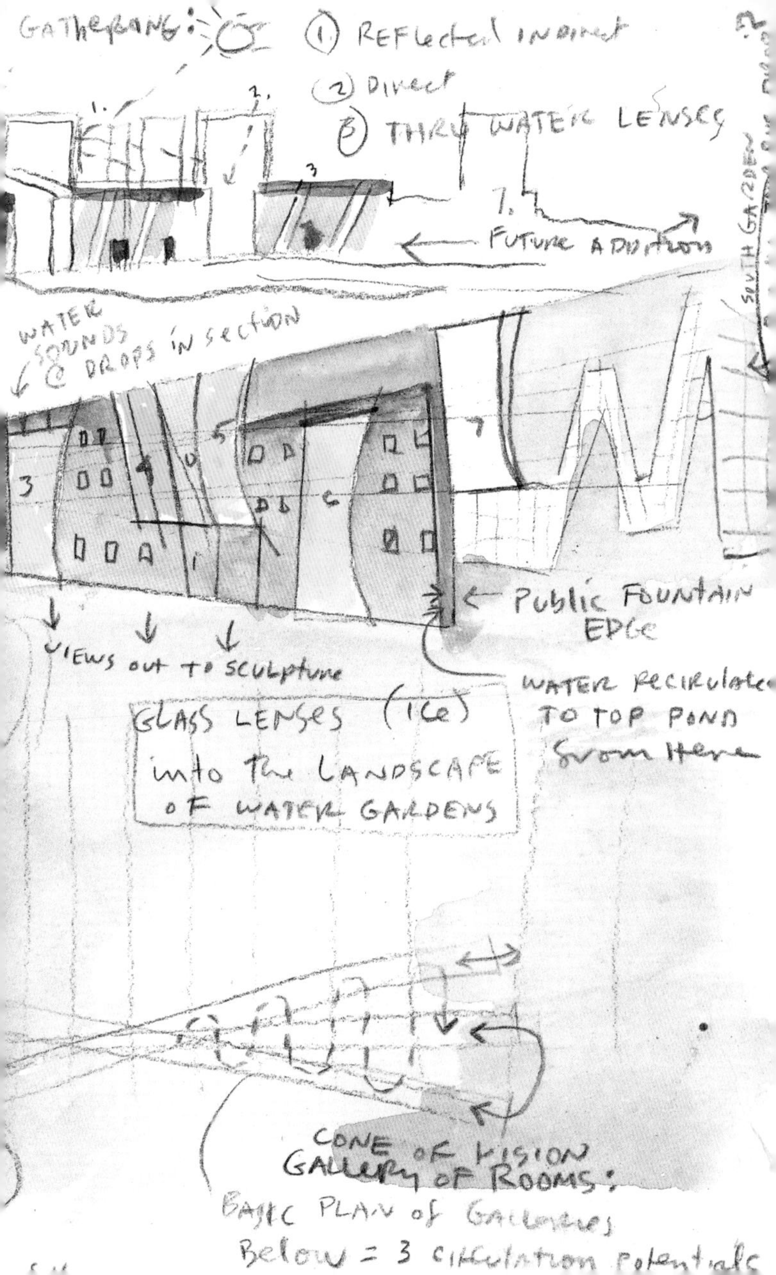

GATHERING: ☼ ① REFLECTED INDIRECT
② DIRECT
③ THRU WATER LENSES

1. ← FUTURE ADDITIONS

SOUTH GARDEN

WATER SOUNDS
@ DROPS IN SECTION

3

← PUBLIC FOUNTAIN EDGE

↓ ↓ ↓
VIEWS OUT TO SCULPTURE

GLASS LENSES (ICE)
into the LANDSCAPE
OF WATER GARDENS

WATER RECIRCULATE
TO TOP POND
from Here

CONE OF VISION
GALLERY OF ROOMS:
BASIC PLAN OF GALLERIES
Below = 3 CIRCULATION POTENTIALS

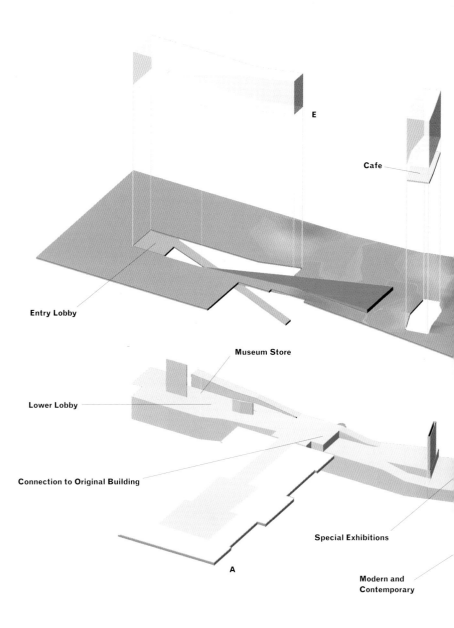

E

Cafe

Entry Lobby

Museum Store

Lower Lobby

Connection to Original Building

Special Exhibitions

A

Modern and
Contemporary

A. Existing Nelson-Atkins
B. Museum expansion of 140,000 sq. ft.
C. Landscape
D. Lenses
E. Entry pavilion

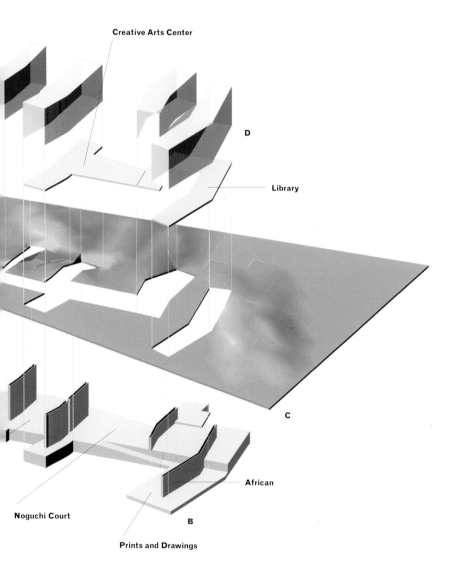

Creative Arts Center

D

Library

C

Noguchi Court

B

African

Prints and Drawings

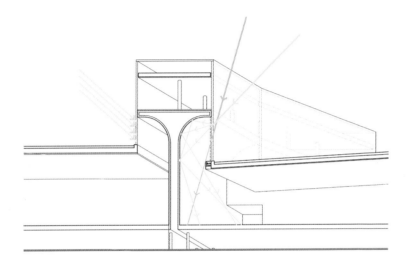

Above: Breathing "T" joins **HVAC** and structural supports for lenses.

Right and following pages: Studies for landscape of lenses

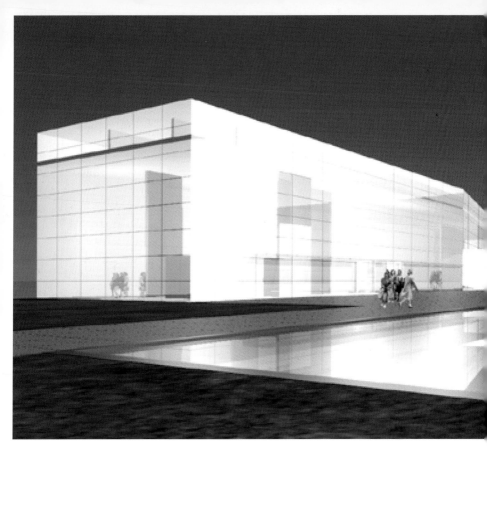

New entry court of lightweight glass and existing stone structure with glass lenses in pond to parking level

Nelson-Atkins Museum Expansion, Kansas City, Missouri, 1999. Light lenses merge with the sculpture garden in complementary contrast to stone 1933 original building.

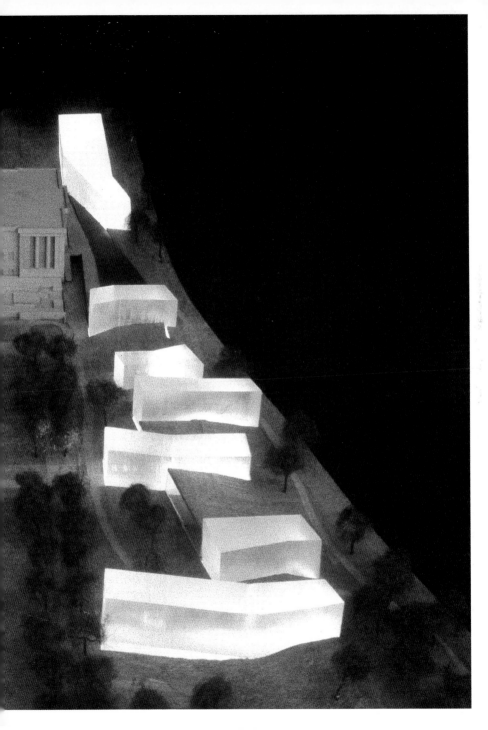

THE STORY OF A STRANGE ATTRACTOR

Like a fly moving through a loop of space, a visitor to the new science museum at the Cranbrook Institute of Science never traces the same path twice. Edward N. Lorenz's diagram describing the concept of "strange attractors" became the concept diagram for our addition to the 1933 Eliel Saarinen-designed museum.

In *Exploring Chaos*, Lorenz states, "Whichever direction you have come from you still have a choice. Moreover, points that start close together get stretched apart as they circulate round the attractor, so they 'lose contact,' and can follow independent trajectories. This makes the sequence of lefts and rights unpredictable in the long term. This combination of factors stretching points apart and 're-injecting' them back into small regions is typical of all strange attractors." (Seattle: University of Washington Press, 1993.)

Edward N. Lorenz's strange attractor diagram, 1968

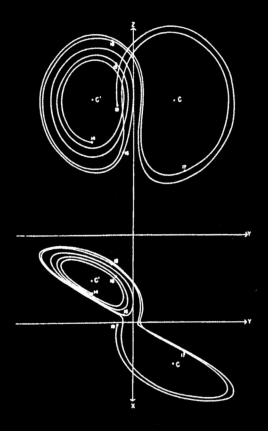

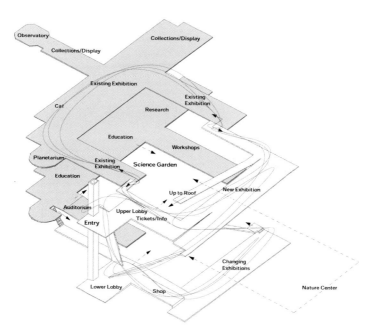

Observatory

Collections/Display

Collections/Display

Existing Exhibition

Existing
Exhibition

Cat

Research

Education

Workshops

Planetarium

Existing
Exhibition

Science Garden

Education

Up to Roof

New Exhibition

Auditorium

Upper Lobby

Entry

Tickets/Info

Lower Lobby

Shop

Changing
Exhibitions

Nature Center

Above: Interlock of old and new building

Right: Cranbrook campus plan with Cranbrook Institute of Science in upper left

The existing U-shaped building had two dead-end galleries classically categorized into Hall of Minerals and Hall of Man. The new slipped U joins the old opening in a series of new loops in space to surround a science garden and relate the exhibits along multiple tangential roots. With this concept as an analog, we made an open-ended addition that can easily adapt to various paths and choices. Alternate circuits offer unique qualities that allow for the potential that no visit to the new science museum is a repeat experience. Each engagement is provocative and unpredictable. The design is as much about the flow of energy as about architectural form.

In the new space formed by the U-shaped, interlocking buildings, what was once an asphalt parking lot is now an enclosed courtyard for a Garden of Science focused on the story of water. The liquid, vapor, and solid states of water are explored in open-air exhibits. The glass bottoms of the flow pools exhibit refraction into the exhibition passage. The House of Vapor and the House of Ice both exhibit the dynamics of chaos. Chaos theory began decades ago in studies of turbulence in water and air.

Study, main exhibit hall

Left: Sloping natural light beam

Above: Passage down to temporary exhibition, sloping floor of permanent exhibition

Streaked sand pattern cast from the sand beach of Lake Superior by Cranbrook Architecture Office

The height and spacing of snow moguls: Multiple generative forces, from the coefficient of friction to the pitch and slope of gravity, yield chaos.

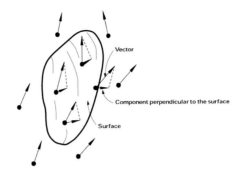

a.

Vector

Component perpendicular to the surface

Surface

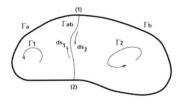

b.

(1)

Γ_a Γ_{ab} Γ_b

Γ_1 ds_1 ds_2 Γ_2

(2)

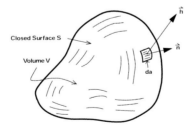

Closed Surface S

Volume V

$\vec{h}$

$\vec{n}$

da

c.

a. The flux of a vector field through a surface is defined as the average value of the normal component of the vector times the area of the surface.

b. The circulation around the whole loop is the sum of the circulations around the two loops.

c. The closed surface S defines the volume V. The unit vector $\vec{n}$ is the outward normal to the surface element da, and $\vec{h}$ is the heat-flow vector at the surface element.

TRIPLENESS

The intersection of art, science, and technology is the mission of the new Bellevue Art Museum, under construction in Bellevue, Washington. It is an open-ended teaching facility with experimental galleries for artists in residence, classrooms, and laboratories. Our first concept for the building focused on the right-hand rule for the direction of charged particles in a magnetic field. This three-pronged diagram, together with the three-part mission, led to studies of "tripleness," or nondialectical ways of seeing and thinking. We envision that fluxes in the new museum will be of both actual and virtual multiplicities.

Below: Concept diagram

Right: Bellevue Art Museum, Bellevue, Washington, 2000. Model of final massing with three galleries and six terraces on the third level.

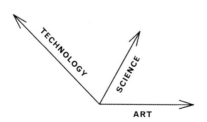

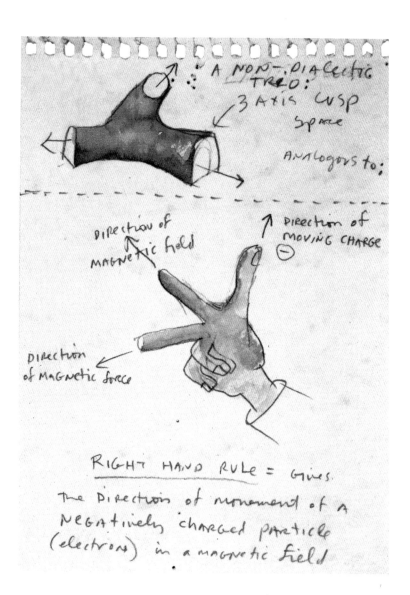

A NON-DIALECTIC TRIO:
3 AXIS CUSP SPACE

ANALOGOUS to:

DIRECTION of MAGNETIC field

DIRECTION of MOVING CHARGE
⊖

DIRECTION of MAGNETIC force

RIGHT HAND RULE = Gives
The DIRECTION of movement of A
NEGATIVELY charged particle
(electron) in a magnetic field

Initial concept drawing

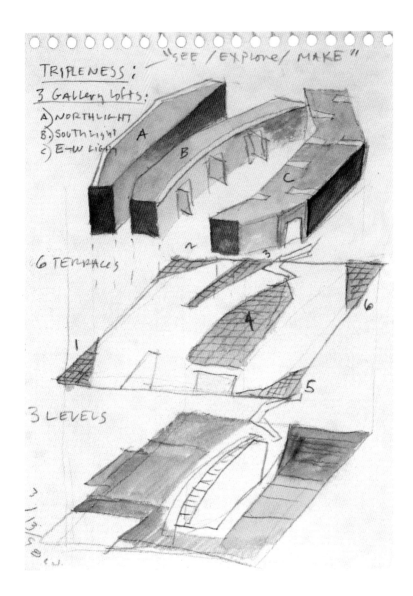

"SEE / EXPLORE / MAKE"

TRIPLENESS:

3 GALLERY Lofts:
A) NORTHLIGHT
B) SOUTHLight
C) E-W Light

A

B

C

6 TERRACES

1 2 3 4 5 6

3 LEVELS

Final concept drawing

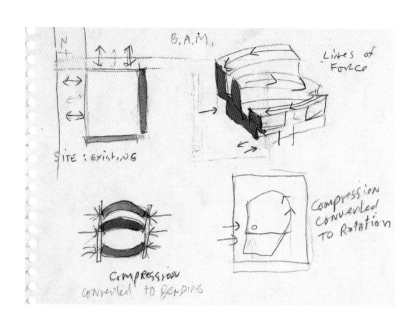

B.A.M.

N

SITE : EXISTING

LINES of FORCE

COMPRESSION converted to BENDING

Compression converted to Rotation

Above: Urban pressure, concrete exterior shear walls with steel inner frames

Right above: South Light Gallery

Right below: North Light Gallery

Terrace of Planetary Motion with *Hubble Telescope* projection showing 56 million light years into space

We expressed the open dynamic of the New City of Culture at Santiago de Compostella, Spain, in fusion plans. The city's institutions are not autonomous entities; they fuse with each other like culture evolves: music with poetry and opera, literature with film and history. Fusion brings the diverse programs of the complex into potential crystallizations with overlapping and flexible connections. Shifts in program coalesce with twists and turns in plan and section.

The expression of one building function distinct from another is synthesized in a translucent glass architecture. The passages and the connections between cultural areas are important catalysts for the design. The Museum of Galicia fuses with the Contemporary Art Museum, the Sound and Image Institute with the Library, in a crossover connection allowing many different programming options for curators and users.

The heart of the New City of Culture is an open center. One enters a monumental space filled with a large central sheet of water open to the sky, framing a view of Santiago de Compostella in the distance. Reflecting the stars and raindrops, this water is the source of five "rivers in reverse," which flow between spaces to form water gardens dedicated to the main Galician cities: La Coruña, Lugo, Orense, Pontevedra, and Santiago de Compostella.

Santiago de Compostella is connected to the New City of Culture by a new pedestrian Ribbon Bridge strung across the valley in a delicate bend. This new link is most vital—an umbilical cord connecting the ancient and the new. Pedestrians arrive at a new sky-lit grotto below the central reflecting pool of the open center. Ceremonial receptions and opening events will take place here.

Fusion plans: In the New City of Culture, different disciplines fuse with each others like culture evolves—music with poetry and opera, literature with film and history.

FUSION — PROGRAM
         SPACE
         TIME

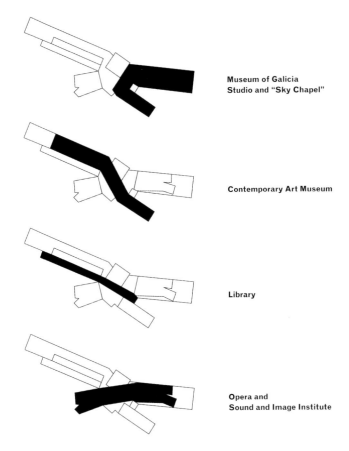

Museum of Galicia
Studio and "Sky Chapel"

Contemporary Art Museum

Library

Opera and
Sound and Image Institute

New City of Culture at the edge of Santiago de Compostella, Spain, 1999

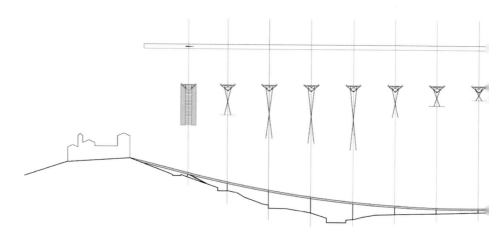

Ribbon Bridge: The old and new cities are connected by a footpath.

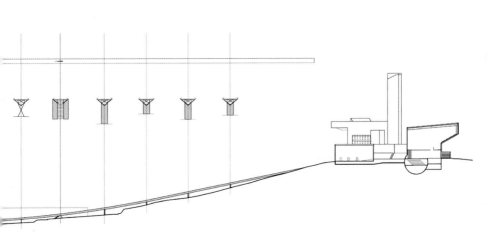

Rather than an acropolis (which transmogrifies into a necropolis), the new city serves as a "catopolis," a catalyst for Galician culture of the past, present, and future. The production of cultural works is driven by the engine of research and teaching areas. A main force of our "engine of culture" concept, the studio tower, contains residential lofts for writers, scholars, composers, and artists. These studios provide a facility to directly invigorate Galician culture. The different disciplines—normally separated in other institutions—are integrated in this central glass tower. At the bottom the tower connects to the Library, Sound and Image Institute, Museum of Galicia, and Contemporary Art Museum, while at the top it rises to a Sky Chapel facing Santiago.

We have envisioned an architecture of clear and translucent white glass emerging from green Galician stone. The double glass walls recycle warm air in winter and cool air in summer. They are not shiny yet they glow invitingly at night. Interior finishes are rich in local materials and also articulate the fusion concept: steel fused with wood (acoustics), stone with silk (cafe), gel with stainless steel (seating), glass with concrete (structure).

The new city forms a landscape rather than objects on a landscape. It is a new terrain fusing water, sky, and gardens. Along the rivers in reverse stone walkways and garden paths lead to open botanical zones where vegetation flourishes. The new city will have a unique architecture: a dynamic expression of fusion with an open center—an engine of culture.

Site photomontage

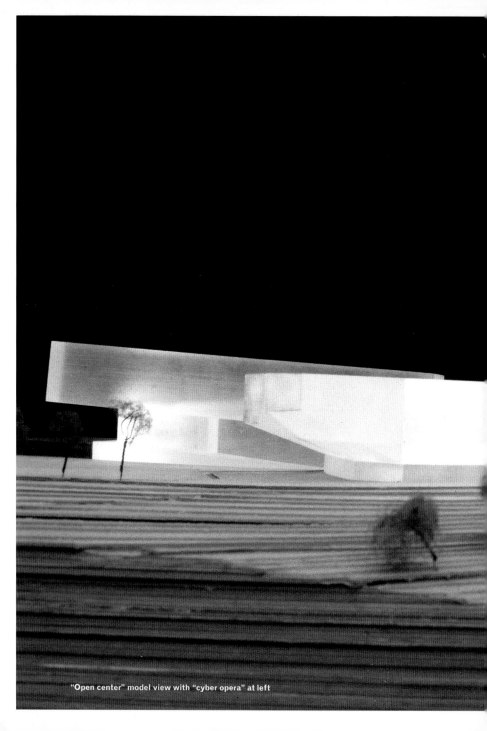

"Open center" model view with "cyber opera" at left

POROSITY
(FROM THE TYPOLOGICAL TO THE TOPOLOGICAL)

In the 1980s, I published little manifestoes in the *Pamphlet Architecture*
series. In two issues, *The Alphabetical City* and *Urban and Rural House
Types*, I argued for reconstructing the city by stark interpretations of type, a
zero ground of architecture.

In 1984, on a long train ride across Canada, a philosophy student introduced
me to the work of Maurice Merleau-Ponty. Critical of the Kantian, the
Bergsonian, and the Sartrean methods, I immediately connected to
architecture in the writings of Merleau-Ponty. I began to read everything
that I could find of his work.

The train trip had a turning point—the "spiral tunnel," a famous construction
through a large mountain. Its spiral space echoed the change in my thinking
from the typological to the topological. The problem with a theory of
architecture that begins in type is the impossible gap between analysis
and synthesis. With the reflective capacities of phenomenology, an intrinsic
understanding of space, and a pure passage from the sign to the signified,
it is possible to move from the particular to the universal. The seer and
the architectural space were no longer opposites; the horizon includes the
seer. A new topological openness in the form of a field that extends to a
"horizon-structure" became my theoretical frame (no longer simple
morphology-typology).

Our book *Questions of Perception: Phenomenology of Architecture* (*A+U*,
1993) is divided into eleven "Phenomenal Zones": 1. Enmeshed Experience:
The Merging of Object and Field; 2. Perspective Space: Incomplete
Perception; 3. Of Color; 4. Of Light and Shadow; 5. Spatiality of Night; 6.
Time Duration and Perception; 7. Water: A Phenomenal Lens; 8. Of Sound; 9.
Detail: The Haptic Realm; 10. Proportion, Scale, and Perception; 11. Site,
Circumstance, and Idea. This book (with contributions by Alberto Perez-
Gomez and Juhani Pallasmaa) broke clear of postmodernism's
countermovement, deconstruction.

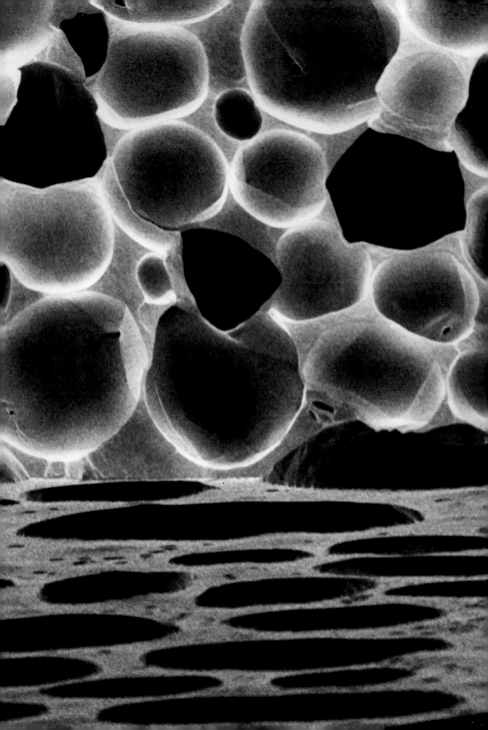

SPONGE FORCE FIELD + ENERGY.

Merleau-Ponty's concepts are pivotal to our architectural methods. As he states, environments include patterns, "lines of force," and—if we can read them—meanings. Focusing on the essential characteristics of a situation and the geometry of a structure creates ways of dealing with problematic elements. For example, what if one aspect of a site—porosity—becomes a concept? Porosity can be a new type of being. Its potentiality of consciousness indicates an opening where the horizon is included within it. We hope to develop the possibility of a collection of things held together in a new way where the "horizon" is open and merges with both exterior and interior.

Left: Study for undergraduate Residence, MIT, Cambridge, Massachusetts, 2001.
Force fields of energy—sponge voids in section.

Below: Natural sponge with grain variations in each face

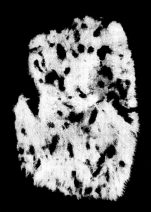

Urban porosity on the 90 x 2000 ft. strip of Vassar Street at MIT
Vertically porous, all-over porous, diagonally and horizontally porous

Our project for an undergraduate residence for 350 students at the Massachusetts Institute of Technology began by rejecting an urban plan that called for a wall of brick buildings of a particular "Boston type." Instead, we argued for urban porosity. Along the 2100-foot strip of Vassar Street, a series of buildings would each demonstrate porosity in four different ways: horizontal, vertical, diagonal, and overall porosity. We developed horizontal porosity in a "folded street" concept that merged 1:20 sloped sections of lounge-corridors with rooms in suspended trusses. After we completed all schematic drawings, we were told that the planning authorities would not allow a building over 100 feet in height. We immediately shifted to another example in our porous urban strip—the sponge—to create overall urban porosity.

The building mass has five large-scale openings, which due to the PerfCon structure require no beam cantilevers. The next scale of openings—the vertical voids—are geometrically developed from ruled surfaces, which vertically connect "sponge paintings" made on every other floor plate. These voids become activist areas of the house lounges and are filled with light and air. The extra-wide main corridors are broken by these vertical voids, like events along a city street.

The 9'-3" height of the ceilings offers the last luxury—the luxury of space. Students will manipulate, pile up, recreate with, and interact with these open volumes. Due to the 20-inch depth of the window wall, summer sun is blocked from entering directly while winter sun is drawn in. Night light from the "sponge" will be an indeterminate urban event, a dynamically random sparkling orchestrated by the students.

Concept diagrams: Urban porosity; individual building porosity

Following page: Diagram of inner voids: sponge painted plans connected by ruled surfaces through two floors

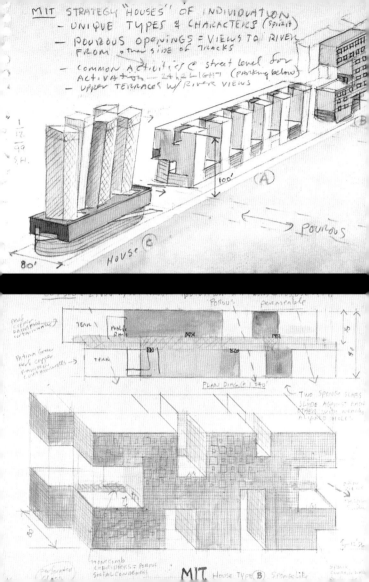

MIT STRATEGY "HOUSES" OF INDIVIDUATION
- UNIQUE TYPES & CHARACTERS (spirit)
- POROUS OPENINGS = VIEWS TO RIVER
  FROM other side of TRACKS
- COMMON Activities @ street level for
  ACTIVATION ——— 24 hr LIGHT (parking below)
- UPPER TERRACES w/ RIVER VIEWS

1
"
40
S.H.

100'   (A)

80'   HOUSE (C)   POROUS

(B)

PROP
COPPER PANELS
PERFORATED
CURTAINWALLS

Patina Green
Perfs copper
Perforated
curtainwalls ——>

TERM   Public Rms   POROUS   PERMEABLE

T FAN

PLAN DIAG (?) 1:40'   TWO SPENSE SLABS
                         SLIDE AGAINST EACH
                         OTHER WITH VARYING
                         ALIGNED HOLES.

88'

Perforated
Glass   HONEYCOMB
           COLUMN BOXES = POROUS
           SPATIAL CONDITIONS

MIT House Type (B) Stone-like

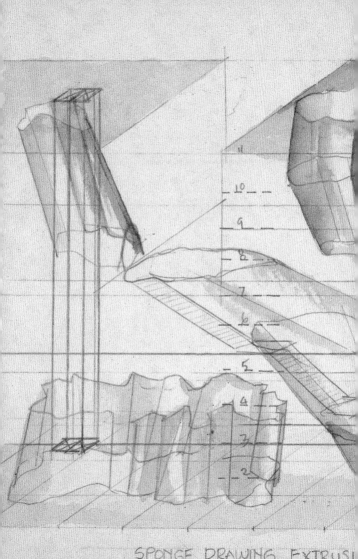

SPONGE DRAWING EXTRUSI

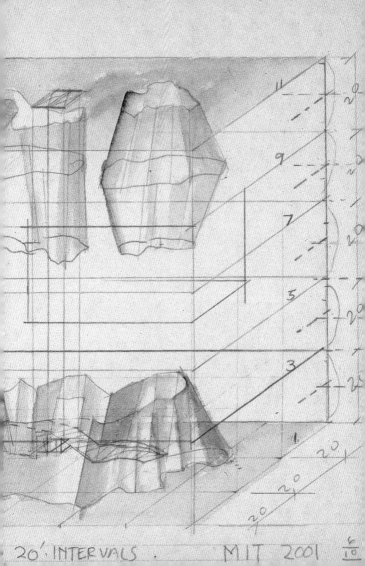

20' INTERVALS . MIT 2001 $\frac{6}{10}$

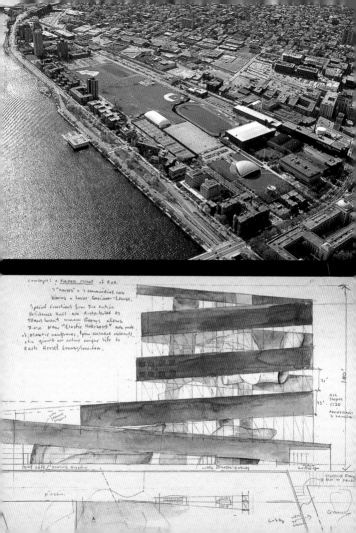

Ruled surfaces connect sponge print plans, forming each of the lounges for the ten houses.

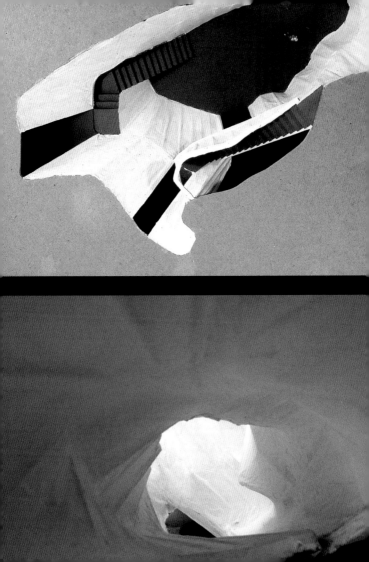

HORIZONTAL POROSITY

In our new addition to the College of Art and Art History on the campus of the University of Iowa, porosity is planar; edges become "fuzzy." The site of the building is adjacent to a lagoon and a limestone cliff. Along the Iowa River, the existing 1937 building is a brick structure with a central body and flanking wings. The Iowa city grid extends across the river to the limestone bluffs, where it breaks up. The new building straddles these two morphologies. A 1960s-era addition to the school extends along the river and joins the original building, covering its river-facing entrance.

Our new building partially bridges the lagoon and partially connects to the organic geometry of the limestone bluff. Its volumes are implied by its outlines. The building is an open instrument, rather than an object. Its flat or curved planes are slotted together or assembled with hinged sections. Flexible spaces open out from studios in warm weather. The school's architecture represents a hybrid vision of the future: half bridge, half loft; half theory, half practice; part technological, part anthropomorphic.

College of Art and Art History, University of Iowa, Iowa City, Iowa, 2000. Site at lagoon.

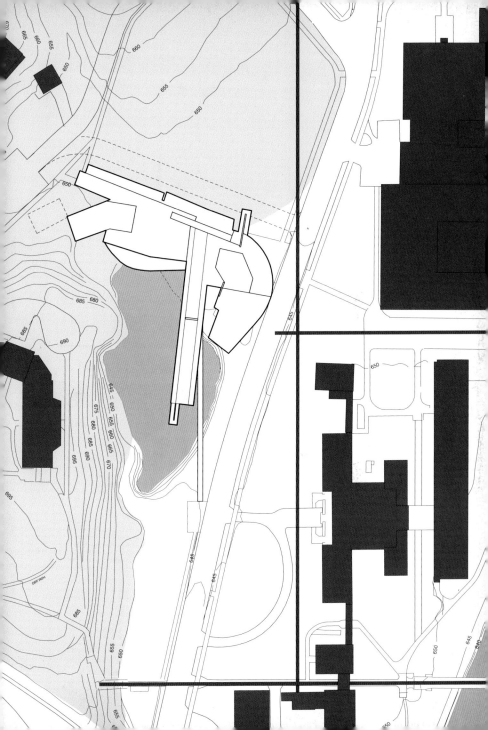

Hybrid bridge-building studies. A series of transformations compared to Picasso's sculpture *Maquette for Guitar* of 1912.

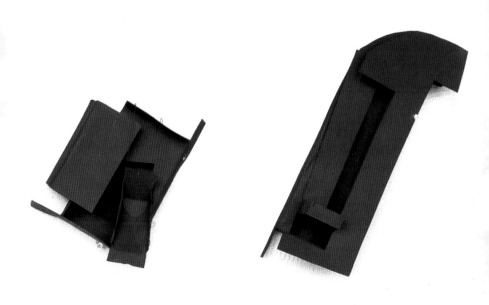

We made our initial study models in a sequence of planar constructions. Six months into the experimental process we began to recognize dynamic geometrical aspects similar to those in Pablo Picasso's rusted sheet metal sculpture *Maquette for Guitar* of 1912. We paused for a morning and built a model version of the sculpture in scaled sequence. Then we moved on to work out the functions further in the hybrid planar architecture. Perhaps the cable-stay steel rods of the bridge in our final design still linger as an "instrument" inspiration.

The main horizontal passages throughout the building are meeting places whose interior glass walls expose ongoing work in progress. The interplay of light and shadow in the interior is controlled with overlapping planes on the exterior. Exposed tension rods on the bridge section contribute to the linear and planar architecture. The interior floors are suspended from the light-capturing planar beams, which also hold the air distribution ducts and fluorescent light pockets.

The architecture of the College of Art and Art History explores "formless" geometries in its disposition of spaces and combinations of routes. As a working and flexible teaching instrument, the building connects interior functions that overlap spatially at its center. Space is envisioned as a social condenser where ongoing work can be observed. Around the perimeter, spaces overlook, overlap, and engage the natural landscape of the surroundings. The dispersion and "fuzziness" of the edges embrace phenomena such as sunlight reflected from water on the lagoon and the up-reflected, white light of freshly fallen snow.

Site model showing existing red brick building. The inscription over the entry reads, *"Ars longa vita brevis est"*—art is long, life is brief.

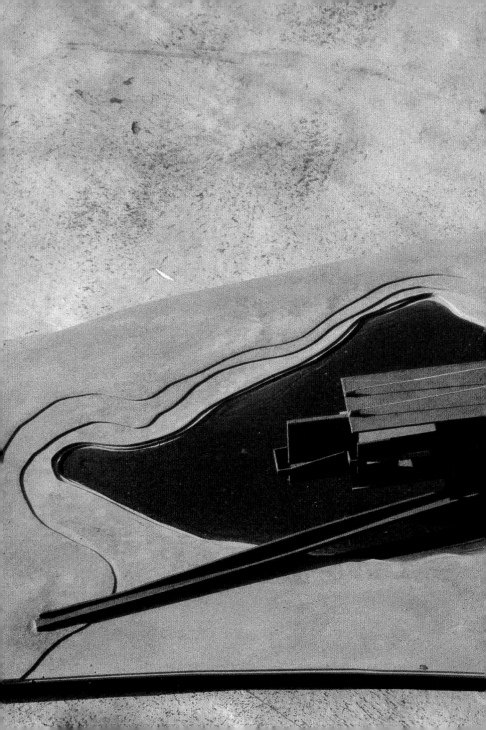

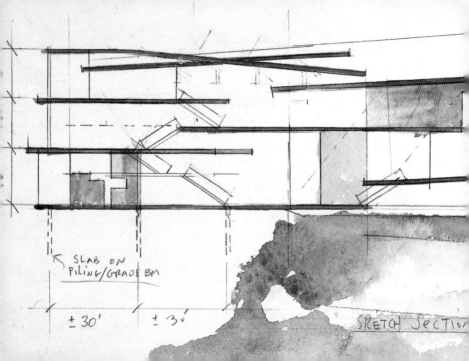

SLAB ON
PILING/GRADE BM

± 30'   ± 30'

SKETCH SECTION

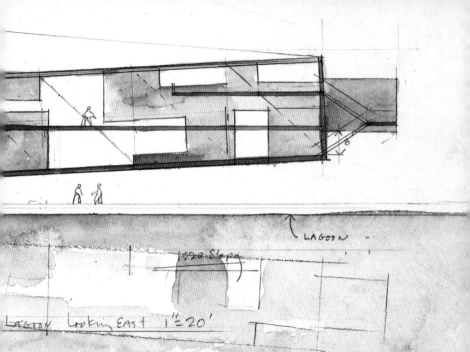

LAGOON

1:20 Slope

LAGOON looking EAST 1"=20'

The principles of the most economical building type in America—the prefabricated steel building—are employed in the building structure and materials. Metal sheets gain strength in folding while using a minimum of material. Steel in suspension is very efficient. Due to their low relative height, interiors gain their character through the composition of exposed steel structure and HVAC systems.

The richness in the architectural language of the building is developed in the inventive use and combination of basic elements. Fluorescent tubes for lighting are hidden by the bottom flange of steel beams while ductwork and steel structure merge into complex compositions.

The red coloring of the new building joins it to the original red brick structure, as does its low landscape-embracing profile. A new facility of inspiring interior spaces and natural light works as an open instrument toward the production of past, present, and future art.

Normative typological objects of architecture are developed in double-loaded corridors and corners. These compositions engage a more porous topological experience of the body moving through space. Such buildings are engaged rather than detached to twilight and crickets in Iowa or moonlight and women's volleyball along the Charles River; the hope is to make them new topological spaces that activate and inspire.

Right: Planar structure in raw steel filled with concrete at columnar positions

Following page: Enlarged study of steel planar space and structure

IOWA. 10/27/59

EDGE OF A CITY

"Lived together in streets, plazas, buses, taxis, movie houses, theaters, bars, hotels.... The enormou city that fits in a room three yards square, and endless as a galaxy."

—Octavio Pa

There is fatigue in urban planning ideas today. We see old academic planners making reports, maps, and long-range plans that are ignored by high-paced, capitalist development. Real effects on the urban framework are caused by intelligent constructions that, when realized, act as a catalyst for alternatives. The skin of the world measures every building plan. In the last few decades negative changes—more species extinction and habitat destruction than in the previous million years—have forced action. The issues of urban planning remain as crucial as ever, thus requiring new strategies and new enthusiasm.

In the twenty-first century, we must consider visions of cities from the point of view of the landscap New types of urban spaces—great cities that coexist with preserved natural landscapes—should be our first priority.

On the fringe of the modern city, displaced fragments sprout without intrinsic relationships to the existing organization, other than that of the camber and loops of the curvilinear freeway. Here, the thrown-away spreads itself outward like the nodal lines of a stone tossed into a pond. The edge of a city is a philosophical region where city and natural landscape overlap and exist without choice or expectation. This zone calls for visions and projections that delineate the boundary between the urban and the rural. Visions of a city's future can be plotted on this partially spoiled land in order to liberate the remaining natural landscape and protect the habitats of hundreds of species of animals and plants that are threatened with extinction. What remains of the wilderness can be preserved; defoliated territory can be restored. In the middle zone between landscape and city, there is hope for a new synthesis of urban life and urban form. Traditional planning methods are no longer adequate to address this edge.

Is sprawl a spontaneous spreading of democracy or the political accumulation of unprecedented ignorance? The freedom of expression of a strong economy can take many other forms. In order to keep the low density of the rural and high density of the urban while reducing the proliferation of the suburban, new strategies ought to begin with public education. A new study of 245 endangered or recently extinct species around the world demonstrates that a population headed toward extinction does not respond by contracting inward. Human-provoked destruction of habitat and pollution overwhelms the natural tendency of a population to contract inward; survivors gather on the edges, at high elevations or isolated in pockets. Peripheral landscapes may be the future places in which to keep species alive.

Pedestrian intersection

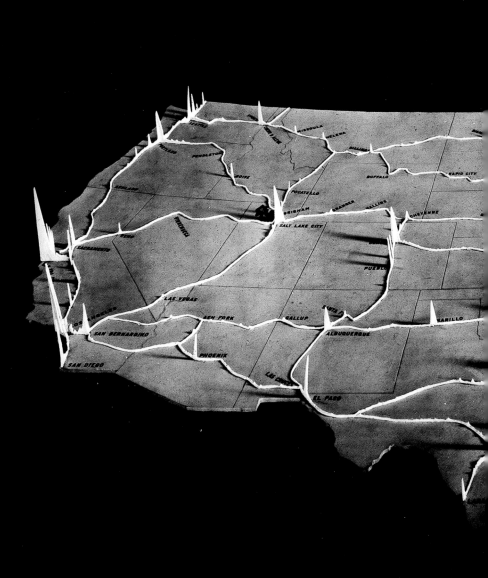

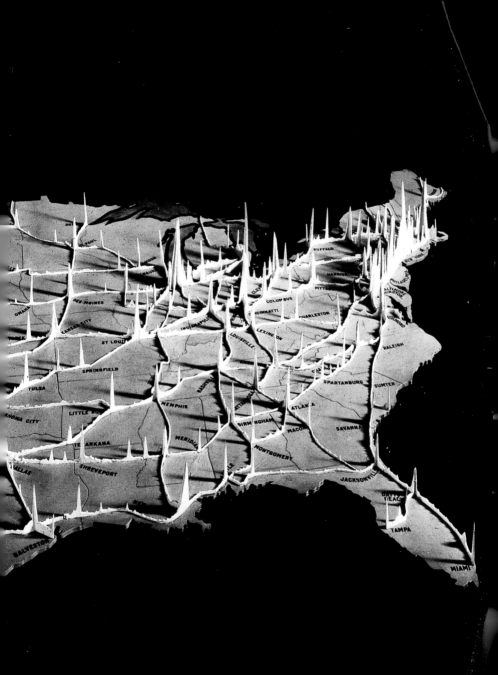

1930 traffic pattern across landscape; there were 26,749,853 cars in the U.S., today there are 250 million.

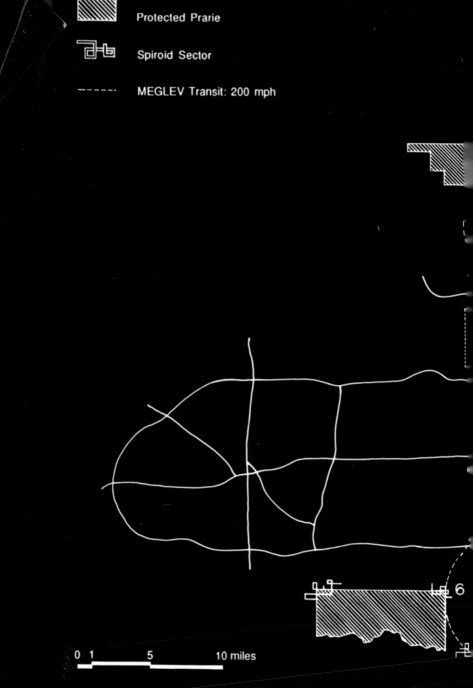

Protected Prarie

Spiroid Sector

MEGLEV Transit: 200 mph

0 1   5   10 miles

Dallas/Fort Worth Spiroid Sectors, 1989, connected by Meglev in north/south loop via the airport

SEVEN STATIONS:
1.   Black Snake
2.   Anima Mundi
3.   Breakwater
4.   Sanctuary
5.   Campus
6.   Hangdog
7.   Instaneity

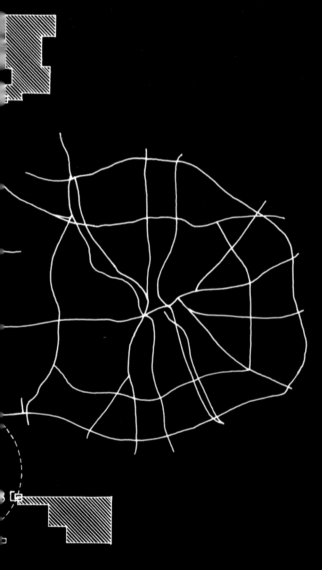

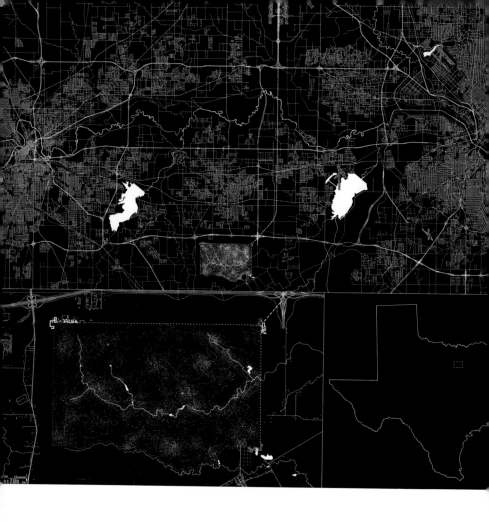

Dallas Spiroid Sectors

Spiroid Sectors bracketing natural landscape, Dallas, Texas, 1989

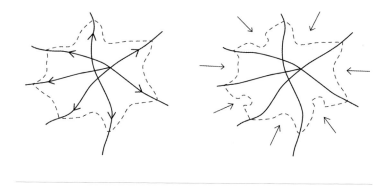

Top: Town—Country : Country—Town. The Process of Conurbation. Diagram from Patrick Geddes's *Cities in Evolution* (1915) showing urban sprawl and its remedy.

Bottom: Peripheral landscapes diagram showing centripetal versus centrifugal movement of endangered species toward peripheral landscapes. Conservation of fauna depends on flora conservation at city edges.

Right: Phoenix Spatial Retaining Bars, 1989

ABSTRACT JOURNEY

"The living have a body which permits them to go out from knowledge and to enter again. They are like a house and a bee."
—Paul Valéry

The path of passage in architecture must lead from the abstract to the concrete, the unformed to the formed. While a painter or a composer might move from concrete to abstract, the architect must travel in the other direction, gradually incorporating human activities into what began as an abstract diagram. Homer's *Odyssey*, written nearly three thousand years ago, is an anthropomorphic account of an abstract idea—in this case the god's concern with the justice of human behavior—working through the lead character as he travels with the sun from east to west, from abstraction to concreteness, from passive observation to action. A text dominated by pathos, despair, and irony, the *Odyssey* can suddenly break into joy and surprise. In Book Five (out of twenty-four), the nymph Calypso (the one who hides?) holds Odysseus at the "navel" of the sea (the island of Ogygia) for seven years; the episode is a mythic allegory of desire. In the end Odysseus refuses Calypso's offer of immortality and continues his journey. It is not what an artist accepts, it is what he refuses that defines the work's meaning.

Homer's ancient epic poem reasserts the paradox of timeless reality. Paradigms of the world have taken radically different modes of discourse since Homer. Yet a world of electronic interaction, microelectric and digital, still requires poetry of ideas. Poetic action is the penultimate in what can be savored.

An intellectual concept (the act) starts as an interaction of the mind and an idea aimed at a process of crystallization. A clear intention can interconnect a manifold of ambiguous roots so that they develop toward an increasingly clear meaning, however abstract. Twenty-first century architecture might act as a cultural neologist; just as new words do, architecture's spatial forms yield new sense experiences or new meanings. Yet a spiritual eponym stands as a shadow, almost a double of the new: there are no elders to carry the burden of moving the work of spirit forward.

When we are at the beginning of a journey we, like Odysseus, contemplate a character (or concept) that does not yet exist. Absence and loss precede the appearance of an abstract driving force. Chaos, confusion, and implosion of information bound up in rules, constraints, and limited means precede every architectural challenge. Once the imagined concept takes hold, its correctness is tested in the way it can work in different modes, from program to light, to space and to material. The journey from the abstract to the concrete is a metamorphosis from a poetic idea with an exploratory diagram, a coherent purpose to form.

Concepts, the tools one uses to drive design, transcend ideological arguments. We work from a limited concept, unique for each site and circumstance. The limited concept gives us the freedom to work within the contingent and uncertain. It is a strategy designed to raise architecture's expressions to a level of thought. Limited concepts aim at fusion: instead of a philosophy about architecture, they lead to architecture that embodies philosophy.

The next stage of the abstract journey is a story within a story. Here the account breaks the horizon of tradition using the technological means at hand and beyond. This electronic and globally transforming moment would revolutionize if it were not so hopelessly lopsided. From the standpoint of project and society, architecture is a story within a story. The smaller story, for example 5% of the larger story, maintains 95% of the means to live and build. The larger story is of the mammoth portion of 6 billion who live in desolate places among forgotten peoples joining a throw-away world. Disproportionately consumed natural resources are violently consumed by the Cyclops of capitalism. The story within a story is reflected from here, not an exclusive position; and yet if there are two societies both depart from the shadows of overreaching technology. The journey within a journey moves toward the transparent and the hyperrealistic. It is a meandering phase; the seen and the unseen appear as revelations and abominations.

Odysseus on his homemade raft faced a sea horizon wrapping 360 degrees. He would hold up one finger against the horizon, look at it first with one eye and then with another. His finger's two positions bracketed a piece of the horizon. When he fully extended his arm and tried this exercise again, a smaller piece of the horizon was bracketed...the parallax was changed! Astronomers long used the same phenomena to measure the distance to the stars. The Earth's orbit around the sun, 186 million miles, was the parallax baseline.

Today the baseline is no longer fixed, our point of view has changed, we see and experience things differently, old words take on new meanings. But the paradox of parallax remains in the seeing self who, in moving, changes the perspective...that is, changes the things seen. Without distrusting the rational potential of thought the senses reveal another world. This phenomenal world is the transfigured world of architecture.

Time, turning in a wide spiral back over itself, torques the clock of the third stage of the abstract journey. Brain-racking digital spaces, topological experiments, slide over the poetic simplicity of Euclid's 2300-year-old *Elementa Geometricae*. The law of chaos is wedded to fissures in time where distant pasts are connected to distant futures. Meaning is criss-crossed and linked, not yielding to the straight line time troubled to produce. Eternal returns do not quite hold as an uplifting angle spiraling off-center slips into the past, breaking again toward the future, cross-fertilized continuously. We escape academic philosophy and scholasticism, being reeducated in thousands of turns on the spiral of action. Architecture's spatial radiance concretizes our dreams, forcing us to transcend what we knew while opening unexpected, sometimes disturbing, if not elastic, horizons.

Architecture is above all very fragile in its inception. It must be nurtured and cultivated. The crunching iron shoes of public opinion can easily end the journey. An oblivion of bureaucracy or insensitive word blasts can crush its preliminary phases. The journey from the abstract requires extraordinary commitment and belief. To realize an individual abstract vision demands even more audacious desire. Twenty-four times rejected, still we hope one more time to be accepted. Amazingly we build something! Inspiring strategies animate space and light endowed with a vital program. Drawers of drawings of buildings unrealized give way to a concrete vision. For some unknowing soul in the future, architecture will spatially arouse, new feelings will be discovered. The journey will begin anew.

Right: Greenhouse effect on Venus—heat image with infrared radiation shining through clouds

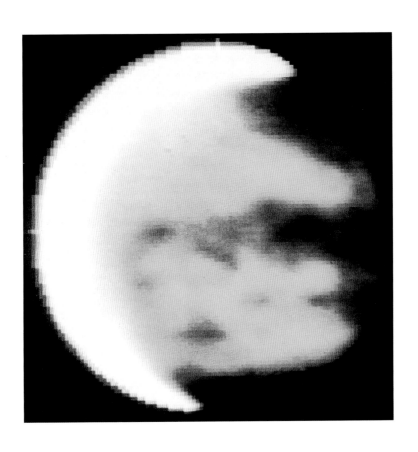

INDEX

UNDERGRADUATE RESIDENCE, MIT
CAMBRIDGE, MASSACHUSETTS, 2001

Following our concept of porosity, we envisioned the 350-bed
Undergraduate Residence as part of both the campus form and city
form. It is a vertical slice of a city 10 stories tall and 330 feet long. This
urban concept provides students with amenities such as a 125-seat theater and a nighttime cafe. The residences' dining hall is on the street
level, like a street-front restaurant with a special awning and outdoor
tables. The eleven-feet-wide corridors connecting the rooms are like
streets that happen upon urban experiences. As in Alvar Aalto's Baker
House across the green, the hallway here is more like a public place, a
lounge, than a mere means of access.

The porosity concept gives the new residence a spongelike building
morphology via a series of programmatic and biotechnical functions.
The overall building mass has five large-scale openings. These roughly
correspond to main entrances, view corridors, and the main outdoor
activity terraces of the dormitory, which are connected to programs
such as the gymnasium. The next scale of openings—a ruled surface
system freely connected to sponge prints, plan to section—creates
vertical porosity in the block. These large, dynamic openings (roughly
corresponding to the "houses" in the dorm) are the lungs of the building,
bringing natural light down and moving air up through the section.

The "PerfCon" structure of the residence is a unique design, allowing for
maximum flexibility and interaction. Each of the dormitory's single
rooms has nine operable windows over two feet square. Due to the thickness of the exterior wall, summer sunlight is blocked while winter sunlight is drawn in.

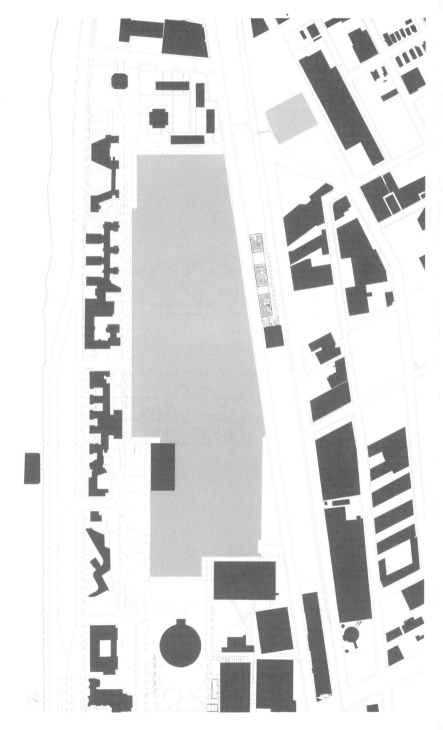

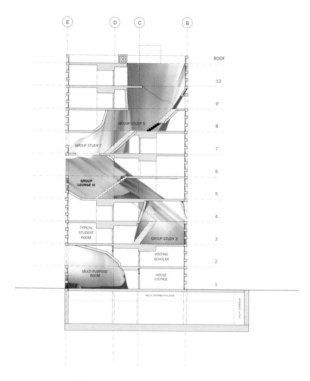

E   D   C   B

ROOF

10

9

GROUP STUDY 9

8

GROUP STUDY 7

7

6

GROUP
LOUNGE III

5

4

TYPICAL
STUDENT
ROOM

GROUP STUDY 3

3

VISITING
SCHOLAR

2

MULTI PURPOSE
ROOM

HOUSE
LOUNGE

1

MECH DISTRIBUTION ZONE

③ NORTH-SOUTH SECTION LOOKING WEST

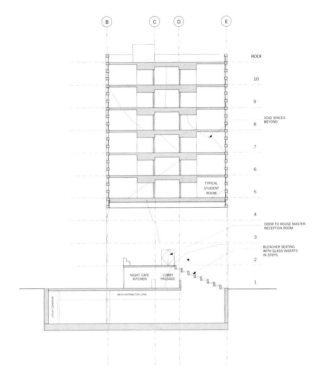

B   C   D   E

ROOF

10

9

VOID SPACES
BEYOND

8

7

6

TYPICAL
STUDENT
ROOM

5

4

DOOR TO HOUSE MASTER
RECEPTION ROOM

3

BLEACHER SEATING
WITH GLASS INSERTS
IN STEPS

2

NIGHT CAFE
KITCHEN   LOBBY
PASSAGE

1

MECH DISTRIBUTION ZONE

UTILITY CORRIDOR

2   NORTH-SOUTH SECTION LOOKING EAST

PALAZZO DEL CINEMA
VENICE, ITALY, 1990

The connection of the Lido site of the project to Venice by water is emphasized by a grand space of arrival on the lagoon. This space, filled with diaphanous light—an homage to Venice—from gaps between the cinemas above, would also be a place for the Lido community. During the months when there is no cinema festival, this public grotto might have shops along the arcade or marina functions.

Time in its various abstractions links architecture to the cinema. The project involves three interpretations of time and light in space. Collapsed time and extended time within cinema—the ability to depict twenty years in one minute or four seconds in twenty minutes—is expressed in the warp and extended weave of the building. Diaphanous time is reflected in sunlight dropping through fissures between the cinemas into the lagoon basin below. Ripples of water and reflected sunlight animate the grand public grotto. Absolute time is measured in a projected beam of sunlight that moves across the "cubic Pantheon" in the lobby. The projections of light in space, in reflection, and in shade and shadow are seen as programmatic aspects to be achieved parallel to solving functional aspects.

A vessel for "filmic time" and "filmic space," the building's perimeter is bottle shaped with its mouth open to the lagoon towards Venice. The cinemas interlock within this frame, creating essential crevices and fissures that allow sunlight to the water below. In section, the cinemas turn slightly, like interlocking hands changing their interior and exterior aspects of space.

In some areas the cinema screens can be withdrawn and the cinema images projected onto warped concrete planes of the structure to appear as dissected colors and light on the exterior. The monolithic red patina of the exterior is interrupted by these warped projection zones. Here cinema burns holes in architecture.

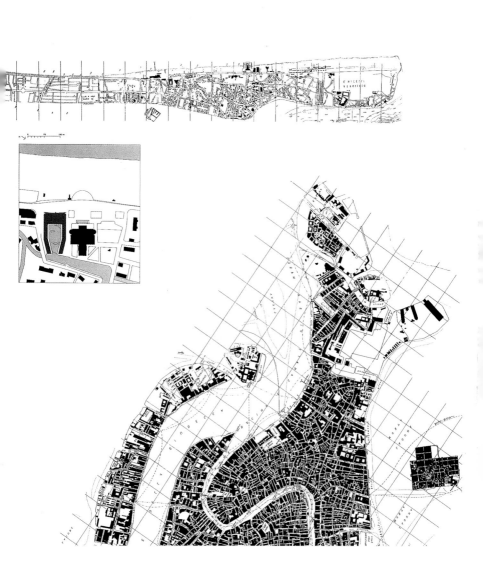

KIASMA MUSEUM OF CONTEMPORARY ART
HELSINKI, FINLAND, 1998

The concept of Kiasma involves intertwining the building's mass with the geometry of the city and landscape, which are reflected in the shape of the building. An implicit "cultural line" curves to link the building to Alvar Aalto's Finlandia Hall while it also engages a "line of nature" connecting it to the adjacent landscape and Töölo Bay.

We created a language of silence by eliminating the intermediate scale in the building's architecture. Artwork can occupy the intermediate scale. Rather than articulating columns, moldings, window openings, etc., we expressed the architecture through details such as the twist of a door handle, the edge of a stair, and the exposed thickness of a slab of glass.

Asymmetry defines movement through a series of spatial sequences, such that the overall design becomes a slightly warped gallery of rooms. These curved unfolding sequences provide elements of both mystery and surprise, which do not exist in a typical single- or double-loaded orthogonal arrangement of spaces. Instead, the visitor is confronted with a continuous unfolding of changing perspectives that connect the internal experience to the overall concept of intertwining.

A common dilemma in the design of an art museum with galleries on multiple levels is that the stacked section only permits natural light to enter the upper level galleries, leaving the lower levels exclusively dependent on artificial light. But Kiasma takes advantage of Helsinki's horizontal natural light. The slight variation in room shape and size due to the gently curving sections of the building allows natural light to enter in different ways. First, the curved "wall of ice" allows vertical light to penetrate through glass planks while horizontal light is deflected through the center section. Thus natural light is able to penetrate both upper and lower levels. Second, the curved roof section with its "bow tie" skylights distributes light to galleries below the top level. The building's curving and intertwining morphology, the interwoven torsion of space and light, have allowed for the twenty-five galleries to be lit naturally.

PROJECT CREDITS

POOL HOUSE AND SCULPTURE STUDIO
Program: Sculpture studio and bathhouse sited next to
an existing pool
Client: Rosen family
Design Architect: Steven Holl
Project team: Mark Janson, James Rosen
Location: Scarsdale, New York
Gross floor area: 682 sq. ft.
Status: Completed 1981

PORTA VITTORIA
Program: Redevelopment of disused freight rail site
Client: XVII Triennale of Milan
Design Architect: Steven Holl
Project Architect: Peter Lynch
Project team: Jacob Allerdice, Laurie Beckerman,
Meta Brunzema, Stephen Cassell, Gisue Hariri, Mojgan
Hariri, Paola Iacucci, Ralph Nelson, Ron Peterson,
Darius Sollohub, Lynette Widder
Location: Milan, Italy
Status: Designed 1986

XYZ APARTMENT, MOMA TOWER
Program: Apartment interior
Design Architect: Steven Holl
Project Architect: Peter Lynch
Project team: Ralph Nelson, Stephen Cassell
Location: New York, New York
Gross floor area: 1,800 sq. ft.
Status: Completed 1987

MARTHA'S VINEYARD HOUSE
Program: Residence
Client: Steven Berkowitz, Janet Odgis
Design Architect: Steven Holl
Project team: Peter Lynch, Ralph Nelson, Peter
Shinoda, Stephen Cassell
Location: Martha's Vineyard, Massachusetts
Net floor area: 2,800 sq. ft.
Status: Completed 1988

SPATIAL RETAINING BARS
Program: Housing, work space, shops
Design Architect: Steven Holl
Project team: Peter Lynch, Pier Copat, Ben Frombgen,
Janet Cross
Location: Phoenix, Arizona
Status: Designed 1989

SPIROID SECTORS
Program: Hybrid building of living quarters
and workplaces
Design Architect: Steven Holl
Project team: Tod Fouser, Peter Lynch, Scott Enge,
Hal Goldstein, Chris Otterbine, Laura Briggs,
Janet Cross
Location: Dallas/Fort Worth, Texas
Status: Designed 1990

VOID SPACE/HINGED SPACE HOUSING
Program: 28 apartments, 7 shops
Client: Fukuoka-Jishu Co., Japan
Design Architect: Steven Holl
Project Architect: Hideaki Ariizumi
Project team: Peter Lynch, Thomas Jenkinson,
Pier Copat
Location: Fukuoka, Japan
Net floor area: 4,243 sq. m.
Status: Completed March 1990

PALAZZO DEL CINEMA
Program: An invited competition for the rebuilding
of the Venice Film Festival Building on the Lido
Client: Venice Biennale
Design Architect: Steven Holl
Project team: Peter Lynch, Steven Cassell,
Janet Cross, Jun Kim, and Adam Yarinsky
Location: Venice, Italy
Net floor area: 120,000 sq. ft.
Status: Competition entry completed May 1990

STRETTO HOUSE
Program: Private residence for art collectors
Design Architect: Steven Holl
Project Architect: Adam Yarinsky
Project team: Peter Lynch, Bryan Bell, Matthew
Karlen, William Wilson, Stephen Cassell, Kent Hikida,
Florian Schmidt, Thomas Jenkinson, Lucinda Knox
Location: Dallas, Texas
Gross floor area: 7,500 sq. ft.
Status: Completed 1992

D. E. SHAW OFFICES
Program: Office and trading area
Client: D. E. Shaw & Co.
Design Architect: Steven Holl
Project Architect: Thomas Jenkinson
Project team: Scott Enge, Tomoaki Tanaka,
Todd Fouser, Hideaki Ariizumi, Annette Goderbauer,
Adam Yarinsky
Location: New York, New York
Net floor area: 10,561 sq. ft.
Status: Completed 1992

STOREFRONT FOR ART AND ARCHITECTURE
Program: Facade renovation for architecture gallery
Client: StoreFront for Art and Architecture,
Kyong Park and Shirin Neshat, directors
Project Architect: Steven Holl with artist Vito Acconci
Fabricator: Face Fabrications
Curator: Claudia Gould
Location: New York, New York
Status: Completed 1993

KNUT HAMSUN MUSEUM
Program: Historical museum including exhibition
areas, a library, a reading room, a cafe, and a 250-seat
auditorium
Client: Hamsun Center
Design Architect: Steven Holl